ECDL

for Microsoft Office 2000

Information and
Communication

ECDL3

module 7

for Microsoft Office 2000

Brendan Munnelly and Paul Holden

Information and Communication

*Everything you need to pass the European
Computer Driving Licence®, module by module*

An imprint of **Pearson Education**

London · New York · Sydney · Tokyo · Singapore ·
Madrid · Mexico City · Munich · Paris

PEARSON EDUCATION LIMITED

Head Office:
Edinburgh Gate
Harlow CM20 2JE
Tel: +44 (0)1279 623623
Fax: +44 (0)1279 431059

London Office:
128 Long Acre
London WC2E 9AN
Tel: +44 (0)20 7447 2000
Fax: +44 (0)20 7240 5771

Website: www.it-minds.com

This edition published in Great Britain in 2002
First published in Great Britain in 2002 as part of *ECDL3 The Complete Coursebook for Microsoft Office 2000*

© Rédacteurs Limited 2002

ISBN 0-130-35464-3

British Library Cataloguing in Publication Data
A CIP catalogue record for this book can be obtained from the British Library

'European Computer Driving Licence' and ECDL and Stars device are registered trademarks of the European Computer Driving Licence Foundation Limited. Rédacteurs Limited is an independent entity from the European Computer Driving Licence Foundation Limited, and not affiliated with the European Computer Driving Licence Foundation in any manner.

This book may be used in assisting students to prepare for the European Computer Driving Licence examination. Neither the European Computer Driving Licence Foundation Limited, Rédacteurs Limited nor the publisher warrants that the use of this book will ensure passing the relevant examination.

Use of the ECDL-F approved Courseware logo on this product signifies that it has been independently reviewed and approved in complying with the following standards:

Acceptable coverage of all courseware content related to ECDL syllabus Module 7 version 3.0. This courseware material has not been reviewed for technical accuracy and does not guarantee that the end user will pass the associated ECDL Examinations. Any and all assessment tests and/or performance based exercises contained in these Modular books relate solely to these books and do not constitute, or imply, certification by the European Driving Licence Foundation in respect of any ECDL examinations. For details on sitting ECDL examinations in your country please contact the local ECDL Licensee or visit the European Computer Driving Licence Foundation Limited web site at http://www.ecdl.com.

References to the European Computer Driving Licence (ECDL) include the International Computer Driving Licence (ICDL).

ECDL Foundation Syllabus Version 3.0 is published as the official syllabus for use within the European Computer Driving Licence (ECDL) and International Computer Driving Licence (ICDL) certification programmes.

Rédacteurs Limited is at http://www.redact.ie

Brendan Munnelly is at http://www.munnelly.com

10 9 8 7 6 5 4 3 2 1

Typeset by Pantek Arts Ltd, Maidstone, Kent.
Printed and bound in Great Britain by Ashford Colour Press, Gosport, Hampshire.

The Publishers' policy is to use paper manufactured from sustainable forests.

Preface

The European Computer Driving Licence (ECDL) is an internationally recognized qualification in end-user computer skills. It is designed to give employers and job-seekers a standard against which they can measure competence – not in theory, but in practice. Its seven Modules cover the areas most frequently required in today's business environment. More than one million people in over fifty countries have undertaken ECDL in order to benefit from the personal, social and business advantages and international mobility that it provides.

In addition to its application in business, the ECDL has a social and cultural purpose. With the proliferation of computers into every aspect of modern life, there is a danger that society will break down into two groups – the information 'haves' and the information 'have nots'. The seven modules of the ECDL are not difficult, but they equip anyone who passes them to participate actively and fully in the Information Society.

The ECDL is not product-specific – you can use any hardware or software to perform the tasks in the examinations. And you can take the seven examinations in any order, and work through the syllabus at your own pace.

This book is one of a set of seven, each dealing with one of the ECDL modules. While each book can be used independently, if you are new to computers,you should read Module 2, *Using a Computer and Managing Files,* before this one. Module 2 teaches you the basic operations that are needed in the other practical modules.

The examples in these books are based on PCs (rather than Apple Macintoshes), and on Microsoft software, as follows:

- Operating system: Microsoft Windows 95/98
- Word Processing: Microsoft Word 2000
- Spreadsheets: Microsoft Excel 2000
- Databases: Microsoft Access 2000
- Presentations: Microsoft PowerPoint 2000
- Information and Communication: Microsoft Internet Explorer 5.0 and Microsoft Outlook Express 5.0

If you use other hardware or software, you can use the principles discussed in this book, but the details of operation will differ.

Welcome to the world of computers!

CONTENTS

Introduction

'The internet is like a library.' You will hear this kind of statement a lot from people who know little about either.

If the internet is a library, it's a strange one indeed. For starters, there is no indexing system. At any rate, the books are not arranged on numbered shelves but scattered on the floor. A lot of what is in the books is untrue, even in the non-fiction ones. There is no librarian, and no information desk. Did we mention also that the lights are turned off?

What's more, you can make as much noise as you like when using the internet, while at the same time collecting facts and figures (and fiction and music and video and sports results and stock prices and weather reports and recipes) from all around the world.

In fact, the principal use of the internet is for e-mail – a way of sending messages from your computer to someone else's computer, whether they are in the next room or in a different hemisphere.

Think of this module as your chance to borrow knowledge and skills you won't ever be asked to return, and to become part of an online electronic community. Welcome to the Internet Age!

CHAPTER 1

Exploring the web

In this chapter

Prepare to take your first steps in exploring the world wide web, or the web, as it is popularly known. In this chapter you will visit and explore websites operated by national newspapers based in Australia, France, Germany and Italy, and by a Paris-based art gallery and an American music store.

Also in this chapter you will learn the basics of operating Internet Explorer, the Microsoft software application for exploring – otherwise known as browsing or surfing – the web.

New skills

At the end of this chapter you should be able to:
- Start Internet Explorer and visit a website
- Explore a website by scrolling down pages and clicking on hyperlinks

- Move backwards and forwards through previously visited web pages
- Open several windows at once in Internet Explorer
- Print web pages, and use the main page setup and print options
- Save text, images, and complete pages from the web
- Access and use Internet Explorer's online help

New words

At the end of this chapter you should be able to explain the following terms:

- Home page
- Address bar
- Website
- Web server
- Web browser

Starting Internet Explorer

Double-click the Internet Explorer icon.
   –or–
   Choose **Start | Programs | Internet Explorer**.
   If your computer has a permanent internet connection, you are ready to surf the web with Internet Explorer.
   If you have a dial-up connection, you must first dial your internet service provider (ISP). Internet Explorer may be set up to do this automatically. If not, you will need to dial your ISP separately.

Internet
Explorer

   Enter your user name and password (if Internet Explorer has not recorded them from the last time that you dialled your ISP), and click **Connect**.

Your browser's start page

Typically, Internet Explorer is set up so that it takes you to a particular web page whenever you start the application.

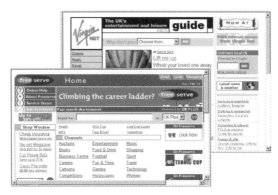

Home pages of two internet service providers (ISPs)

If you obtained Internet Explorer from your ISP, this start page is probably the front page of the ISP's website. Such a front page is called a home page.

Home page
> *The first or front page of a website. Typically, it presents a series of links that you can follow to view the site's other pages.*

You will learn how to change Internet Explorer's start page in Chapter 4.

Visiting and exploring a website

In Exercise 1.1 you visit and explore the website of *The Age*, a newspaper published in Melbourne, Australia.

Exercise 1.1: Visiting and exploring a website

1 Choose **File | Open** or press Ctrl+o.
(That is, hold down the Ctrl key and
press the letter 'o' key.)

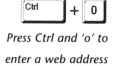

*Press Ctrl and 'o' to
enter a web address*

2 In the Open dialog box displayed, type
www.theage.com.au, and click **OK**.

Internet Explorer displays the
home page of *The Age* website.

Click here

3 Along the left of *The Age's* home
page you can see a list of the
newspaper's main sections –
Today's news, Breaking news,
Photo Gallery, and so on.

Scroll down the page to view the
list in full.

Each section name is underlined, indicating that it is a
hyperlink.

A hyperlink is an item of text (or a graphic) on a web
page that, if clicked, opens another web page, or moves
you to different part of the page that you are on.

Click the section named Today's news.

4 Internet Explorer now displays a new web page, the
Today's news page.

NEWS
Today's news
Breaking news
Features
Photo Gallery
a.m. edition

SPORT
Today's news
Features
SportsToday

TODAY'S NEWS

Yallourn workers return to work

Striking Yallourn Energy workers this evening reluctantly obeyed a return to work order by the State Government, although power restrictions will continue until at least Wednesday. FULL REPORT

Click here

Here you can see summaries of the day's main news stories. Each summary ends with a hyperlink named Full Report.

5 Click on any Full Report hyperlink to display a web page containing an individual news story.

Leave the news story page open on your screen in preparation for Exercise 1.2.

You are now three pages 'deep' inside *The Age* website.

- First, you visited the front or home page.

- Second, you visited the Today's news page, with its list of news summaries.

- Third, you visited a page containing a particular news story.

Internet Explorer toolbar

As with Microsoft Office applications such as Word and Excel, Internet Explorer includes a standard toolbar that offers fast, one-click access to commonly used actions. Rather than introduce all the toolbar buttons at once, we will explain each one as it becomes relevant.

Internet Explorer toolbar

In Exercise 1.2 you will use the
Back and Forward buttons on
Internet Explorer's standard
toolbar.

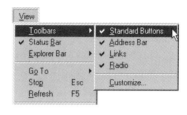

If the Standard toolbar is not
currently shown on your screen,
choose **View | Toolbars | Standard Buttons** to display it.

Moving through a series of web pages

In Exercise 1.2 you learn how to return to web pages that you
visited earlier, and then move forward again to the ones you
visited most recently.

Exercise 1.2: Moving backwards and forwards through web pages

1   With a news story displayed from *The Age*
    newspaper, click once on the Back button,
    located on the left of Internet
    Explorer's Standard toolbar.

    *Returns you to the previously
    displayed web page*

    This returns you to the web
    page you visited most recently – the Today's News page.

2   With the Today's news page displayed, click a second
    time on the Back button.

This returns you to the second-last web page that you visited – the website's home page.

3 With *The Age's* home page displayed, click once on the Forward button. It is located just to the right of the Back button on the Standard toolbar.

Reverses the effect of pressing the Back button

This button moves you forward, one page at a time, retracing your original movement through the website.

4 With the Today's News page displayed, click a second time on the Forward button.

This brings you forward to the web page from which you originally began to move backwards – the individual news story page.

Browsing with the address bar

When you visit a web page, notice that its web address is displayed in the area immediately above Internet Explorer's main window. This is called the address bar.

You can also use the address bar to enter a web address. Although the address bar always displays 'http://' before a web address, you need not type 'http://' when entering an address in the bar.

If the address bar is not currently shown on your screen, choose **View | Toolbars | Address Bar** to display it.

Exercise 1.3: Entering an address in the address bar

1 Click anywhere in the address bar. This selects the currently displayed web address, which is then shown in reverse (white-on-black).

*Removes the character to the **left** of the cursor*

2 Use the Backspace or Delete key to remove the currently displayed web address. The address bar is now empty.

*Removes the character to the **right** of the cursor*

3 Type the following web address in the bar, and click **Go** or press Enter: www.torontostar.ca

Internet Explorer now displays the front page of Canada's *Toronto Star* newspaper.

Practise your web browsing skills by clicking on hyperlinks to display pages of the Toronto newspaper and by scrolling up and down each displayed web page.

Address bar

An area above the main window that shows the address (preceded by 'http://') of the currently displayed web page. You can also use the address bar to enter a web address. (You need not type 'http://'.)

Printing a web page

You can print out the currently displayed web page by choosing **File | Print** and then clicking **OK** on the Print dialog box.

Prints current web page

Alternatively, click the Print button on the Internet Explorer standard toolbar. Clicking this print button does *not* display the Print dialog box.

Page setup options

Internet Explorer's **File | Page Setup** command enables you to control the following:

- **Paper Size**: A4 is a European paper size standard.

- **Orientation**: Portrait ('standing up') or Landscape ('on its side').

- **Print Range**: Your options are: all pages, a specified range of pages, or the part of the page that you have selected.

- **Number of Copies**: If you select any number greater than one, you can specify whether you want the copies collated or not.

- **Margins**: The distance of the page's printed content (text and graphics) from the edge of the paper. You can set each of the four margins (top, bottom, left and right) independently.

- **Header and Footer**: You can include or exclude the following in the header and footer areas of the printed web pages:

- Page title

- Web page address

- Page number in printout

- Total number of pages in printout

- Date of printing

Internet Explorer indicates these options by symbols such as &P and &d. Do you need to remember all these symbols? No; you can refer to Internet Explorer's online help, even during the ECDL test. You will learn about online help at the end of this chapter.

Saving from the web

If you see something on the web that you like – such as an image, some text, or even an entire web page – can you copy it from the website to your computer? Yes. This topic shows you how.

Saving an image

To save an image from the currently displayed web page, right-click on the image to display a pop-up menu. Next, choose **Save Picture As**, select the location on your computer that you want to save to, accept or change the current name of the image, and click **Save**.

Exercise 1.4 provides an example of image saving from the web.

Exercise 1.4: Saving an image from a web page

1 Choose **File | Open** or press Ctrl+o and enter the following web address:

metalab.unc.edu/wm/paint/auth/monet/

Internet Explorer displays the Claude Monet page from the Paris-based webMuseum project.

2 Click on the following hyperlink: Waterlilies

Click here ──────▶

Early works, Sainte-Adresse, near Le Havre 1840-1872
First Impressionist paintings
Later Impressionism
Paris
Rouen Cathedral
• Poplars on the Epte
• Waterlilies
• Haystacks
• Houses of Parliament, London
• Last years

3 On the next web page displayed, click the small picture entitled Water Lilies (The Clouds).

Click here ──────▶

Water Lilies (The Clouds)
1903 (180 Kb); Oil on canvas, 74.6 x 105.3 cm
(29 3/8 x 41 7/16 in); Private collection

Internet Explorer now displays a larger version of the image.

4 When it has displayed fully, right-click anywhere on the image, and choose the **Save Picture As** command from the pop-up menu.

5   In the Save As dialog box then displayed, accept or change the image's file name (monet_wl-clouds.jpg), select the drive and folder you want to save the file to, and click **OK**.

Image file formats

Most image files on the web are in either gif (pronounced with a hard 'g', as in gift) or in jpg (pronounced jay-peg) format.

Selecting and saving text

You can save and reuse all or a selected part of the text from the currently displayed web page. This is a two-step process:

- **Copy**: You select and then *copy* the text to the clipboard, a temporary holding area.

- **Paste**: You *paste* the text from the clipboard into another file, such as a Word document or an Excel spreadsheet.

Four points you should remember about the clipboard:

- The clipboard is temporary. Turn off your computer and the clipboard contents are deleted.

- Text stays in the clipboard after you paste from it, so you can paste the same piece of text into as many different files as you want.

- The clipboard can hold only a single, copied item at a time. If you copy a second piece of text, the second overwrites the first.

- Text copied from a web page and pasted into Word or any other application may lose the formatting that it had on the web.

Exercise 1.5 takes you through the steps of copying and pasting selected text from a web page.

Exercise 1.5: Saving text from a web page

1   Choose **File | Open** or press Ctrl+o, enter the following web address, and press Enter:

www.well.com/user/smalin/miller.html

Here you will find a copy of George A. Miller's classic essay, *The Magical Number Seven, Plus or Minus Two: Some Limits on Our Capacity for Processing Information.*

2   When the web page has loaded fully, scroll down to the end of the page. (A quick way of moving to the bottom of a page is to press Ctrl+End.)

Ctrl + End

Press Ctrl and End to move to the bottom of a web page

Now, press Page Up two or three times until Internet Explorer displays the last paragraph of the essay, which begins with the words 'And finally'.

3   Click at the start of the paragraph and drag the mouse down and right until you have selected the entire paragraph. Your screen should look like that shown.

And finally, what about the magical number seven? What about the seven wonders of the world, the seven seas, the seven deadly sins, the seven daughters of Atlas in the Pleiades, the seven ages of man, the seven levels of hell, the seven primary colors, the seven notes of the musical scale, and the seven days of the week? What about the seven-point rating scale, the seven categories for absolute judgment, the seven objects in the span of attention, and the seven digits in the span of immediate memory? For the present I propose to withhold judgment. Perhaps there is something deep and profound behind all these sevens, something just calling out for us to discover it. But I suspect that it is only a pernicious, Pythagorean coincidence.

When you select text, Internet Explorer displays that text in reverse (white text on black background), rather like the negative of a photograph.

4   Choose **Edit | Copy** or press Ctrl+c to copy the text to the clipboard.

5   Open Microsoft Word, open a new document, and choose **Edit | Paste** or press Ctrl+v to paste the selected text into Word.

When finished, you can close the Word document without saving it, and close Word.

Saving all text

When you want to save *all* the text from a web page, Internet Explorer offers you two options. You can:

• Choose **Edit | Select All**, and then copy the text to the clipboard.

–or–

• Choose **File | Save As**, select the Text File (.txt) option, select the location on your computer that you want to save to, accept or change the default file name, and click **Save**.

Saving a web page

You can save an entire web page – including text, graphics and other components. Exercise 1.6 shows you how.

Exercise 1.6: Saving a web page

1 Visit the MP3 music website at www.mp3.com.

2 Choose **File | Save As**, select the web Page, complete option, select the location on your computer to save to, accept or change the default file name, and click **Save**.

The web page is still on the website. You have saved only a copy of that page on your computer.

Copyright

As you have learnt, it's not difficult to copy text and images from the web to your computer. But it may not always be legal. If you intend reproducing copyright material that you obtained from the web, ask for permission first.

Opening multiple web pages

Internet Explorer allows you to open several web pages at one time. Follow Exercise 1.7 to discover how.

Exercise 1.7: Opening multiple web pages

1   Visit the following website: www.lemonde.fr

Internet Explorer now displays the home page of the French newspaper, *Le Monde*.

2   Choose **File | New | Window** or press Ctrl+n.

Ctrl + N

Press Ctrl and 'n' to open a new window in Internet Explorer

Internet Explorer opens a new, second window. By default, the new window displays whatever web page is shown in the previous one – in this case, the home page of *Le Monde*.

3   Press Ctrl+o and enter www.welt.de, the web address of the German newspaper, *Die Welt*.

DIE ☀ WELT

4   Open a third window, and enter the following web address: www.lastampa.it. This is the home page of the Italian newspaper, *La Stampa*.

LA STAMPA *web*

You can continue to open further windows in Internet Explorer – the only limit on the number of simultaneously open windows is the size of your computer's memory.

5   Close all windows except one. You close a window by
    clicking the Close button at the top-right of the Internet
    Explorer window or by choosing **File | Close**.

Web words

In this chapter we have been using the word 'website'. Let's
look at what this and related terms mean.

The internet or net is an inter-network – a network of
networks. As you may remember from Module 1, a network is
a group of computers (and perhaps other devices such as
printers and scanners) connected together by some means.

On the net, the word *site* is used to describe a single
network. A net site becomes a website when it includes a
computer that acts as a web server. The net existed long
before web servers, and today not every net site includes a
web server.

Website

>   An internet-connected network that is owned and
>   managed by an individual, company or organization, and
>   that includes a web server.

Web servers and web browsers

What's a web server? It's a computer that stores files of a
particular format, and makes them available ('serves them
up') over the internet to computer users who have a software
application called a web browser.

Web server

> *A computer on an internet-connected network that stores files and delivers them over the internet in response to requests from web browsers.*

What's a web browser? It's a software application that sends requests to a web server for files, and then displays the files on the user's screen. Microsoft Internet Explorer and Netscape Navigator are the two most popular web browser applications.

Web browser

> *An application such as Microsoft Internet Explorer that enables a user to request files from a web server over the internet, and displays the requested files on the user's computer.*

Online help

Like Excel, Access, PowerPoint and other Microsoft applications, Internet Explorer offers a searchable online help system:

- The 'help' in online help means that the information is there to assist you to understand and use the application.

- The 'online' means that the material is presented on the computer screen rather than as a traditional printed manual.

You can search through and read online help in two ways: from dialog boxes, or from the **Help** menu.

Using help from dialog boxes

You can access online help directly from a dialog box, as Exercise 1.8 demonstrates.

Exercise 1.8: Using online help in a dialog box

1 Choose **File | Page** Setup to display the Page Setup dialog box.

2 Click the question-mark symbol near the top-right of the dialog box. Internet Explorer displays a question mark to the right of the cursor.

3 Click anywhere in the Header box.

4 Internet Explorer now displays help text telling you about the various header codes.

Practise Exercise 1.8 with other dialog boxes in Internet Explorer.

Using Help menu options

You can also access online help from the **Help** menu. Choose **Help | Contents and Index** to display the three tabs of the Help Topics dialog box.

Contents tab
This offers short descriptions of Internet Explorer's main features.

Where you see a heading with a book symbol, double-click to view the related sub-headings.
Double-click on a question mark symbol to read the help text.

Index tab
*Reading the material displayed on this tab is like looking through the index of a printed book. Just type the first letters of the word or phrase you are interested in. Internet Explorer responds by displaying all matches from the online help in the lower half of the dialog box. When you find the index entry that you are looking for, click the **Display** button.*

Search tab
*Can't find what you are looking for in the Contents or Index tabs? Try this tab. When you type a word or phrase and click **List Topics**, Internet Explorer performs a deeper search of the online help. When you find the item you are looking for, double-click on it to display information about it in the right-hand pane.*

As you search through and read online help topics, you will see the following buttons at the top of the online help window:

- **Hide/Show**: Hides or displays the left-hand pane of the online help dialog box.

- **Back/Forward**: Moves you backwards and forwards through previously visited help topics.

- **Options**: Offers a number of display choices, and enables you to print the currently displayed online help text.

- **Web Help**: Takes you to Microsoft's web-based support site for Internet Explorer.

Take a few minutes to look through Internet Explorer's online help system. Remember that you are free to use online help during an ECDL test.

When finished, you can close Internet Explorer by clicking the Close button or choosing **File | Close**. You have now completed Chapter 1 of the ECDL *Information and Communication* module.

Chapter summary: so now you know

Internet Explorer is a *web browser* application that enables you to request information from *web servers* over the internet.

Internet Explorer typically takes you to a particular web page – called the *start page* – whenever you start the application. If you obtained Internet Explorer from your ISP, the start page is probably the *home page* of your ISP's website.

A home page is the first or front page of a website. Typically, it presents a series of *hyperlinks* that you can follow to view the site's other pages.

You can enter a web address in Internet Explorer using the **File | Open** command, by pressing Ctrl+o, or by typing it in the *address bar*. The address bar, located above the main window, always shows the address of the currently displayed web page.

Along the top of the Internet Explorer window is the *standard toolbar* that gives you one-click access to commonly used browsing actions such as moving back and forwards through previously visited web pages.

You can open *multiple windows* in Internet Explorer at one time, and display different web pages in each one. The application also allows you to save web pages or selected images and text from web pages on your computer.

CHAPTER 2

Finding information within websites

In this chapter

Many websites contain hundreds – even thousands – of pages. The web-based edition of a daily newspaper, for example, typically consists of a hundred pages or more. If a newspaper offers an online archive of past issues over three years, the total number of pages at its website might exceed ten thousand.

Other examples of very large websites include those run by online retailers that stock tens of thousands of music CDs or several million books. Travel and holiday websites can also contain huge numbers of pages offering timetable and destination information.

How do you find particular items of information on such sites? This chapter shows you how.

Also in this chapter you learn about web-address standards and how different countries follow slightly different web-addressing conventions.

New skills

At the end of this chapter you should be able to:

- Find a word or phrase on a web page
- Use a site index to locate information within a website
- Use a search engine to find information within a website
- Use an interactive form to find information within a website
- Describe the web address standards used in the US, the UK, Italy, France, Germany, Australia and South Africa
- Explain how folder and file names are incorporated within web addresses

New words

At the end of this chapter you should be able to explain the following terms:

- Navigation bar
- Keyword
- Website search engine
- Interactive form
- Web address (URL)

Finding text within a web page

To help you find a particular word or phrase on a web page, Internet Explorer provides the **Edit | Find (on this Page)** command. This command searches only:

- The currently *displayed* web page – not the entire website, and not the whole world wide web!

- The currently *loaded* part of the web page. So wait until a page is completely loaded (copied from the website to your computer's memory) before using the command.

Status bar indicates
when web page has ——▶ 🔲 Done   🌐 Internet
fully loaded

- The *text* of the page. Words that are displayed within images are ignored.

Exercise 2.1 shows you how to use this command on a lengthy, text-intensive web page.

Exercise 2.1: Finding information within a web page

1   Open Internet Explorer and visit the web page
    containing George A. Miller's essay, *The Magical Number
    Seven, Plus or Minus Two.* The address is:
    www.well.com/user/smalin/miller.html

2   Choose **Edit | Find (on this Page)** or press Ctrl+f, enter
    the word 'variance' in the Find dialog box, and click
    Find Next.

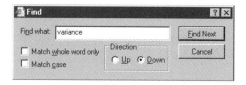

3   Internet Explorer takes you to the first occurrence of the
    word on the web page. The dialog box stays open on
    your screen.

4   To find further occurrences, click **Find Next** again.
    When finished, click **Cancel.**

Finding information within a website

Larger websites can contain many hundreds and even
thousands of individual web pages. To help you locate
particular information, such websites generally offer one or
more of the following three features:

•   **Site index:** Sometimes called a site map or site guide, this
     is a web page that lists the main contents of the website.

- **Search engine**: A program that searches for occurrences of text (words, numbers or other keyboard characters) that you enter, and displays a list of all web pages that contain such text, together with a summary description of each listed page.

- **Interactive forms**: These enable you to request specific information. You will commonly find forms on travel and holiday websites, and on websites that sell highly configurable products (such as computers).

Website index pages

Exercises 2.2, 2.3 and 2.4 provide examples of displaying index pages on three websites – an American software developer (Symantec), a British airline (British Airways) and a British media organization (the BBC).

In each exercise, click on a number of links from the index web page to explore the particular website. And then click the Back button to retrace your steps.

Exercise 2.2: Displaying the index page of a software developer's website

1 Visit the website of Symantec by entering the following address: www.symantec.com

2 Along the bottom of the home page you will see a number of hyperlinks. Click on the one named Site Index.

3 This brings you to Symantec's index page, where you will find a comprehensive listing of the website's contents.

Exercise 2.3: Displaying the index page of an airline website

1 Visit the British Airways website. The address is: www.britishairways.co.uk

Along the top of the home page you will find a link named Site Index.

2 Click it to display the contents of the airline's website.

Exercise 2.4: Displaying the index page of a media website

1 Visit the website of the British Broadcasting Corporation at www.bbc.co.uk

Near the top-left of the home page you will find a link named A-Z index.

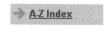

2 Click it to display the contents of the BBC's website.

Some websites display their main links across the top of every page; others list them down one side of the page. A list of the main website links is called a navigation bar or 'navbar'. A navbar may be made up of text or graphics.

Navigation bar

A horizontal or vertical list of hyperlinks to the main components of a website, such as Home (the front page), Site Index (or Site Map or Guide), Company Profile, Products, Services and Staff Contacts.

Site index

Also known as a site map or site guide, this is a web page that lists the main contents of a website.

Website search engines

Site indexes can help you to discover the range and depth of information available on a website. To find one or a few specific items, however, search engines are better.

Exercises 2.5, 2.6 and 2.7 provide examples of search engines on three websites – a film information site (Internet Movie Database), a magazine archive (*The Scout Report*), and an online dictionary of computer terminology (PC Webopedia).

Exercise 2.5: Searching a film database

1 Visit the Internet Movie Database by entering the following address: www.imdb.com

2 In the Search box near the top-left of the home page, enter a film title – for example, Casablanca – and click the **Go!** button.

The IMDB responds by listing pages from its database that relate to your selected film.

Exercise 2.6: Searching a magazine archive

1 Visit *The Scout Report* website. This
   weekly online publication identifies
   and reviews internet resources of
   interest to researchers and educators. Its address is:
   www.scout.cs.wisc.edu/report

2 In the Search box near the top-right of the home page,
   enter a subject in which you are interested – for
   example, botany – and click **Go!**

The Scout Report responds by listing articles from its archives
that relate to your entered topic.

Exercise 2.7: Searching a computer dictionary

1 Visit the PC Webopedia
   website at
   www.pcwebopedia.com

2 In the Search box near the top of the home page, enter
   a term you would like explained – for example, modem
   – and click **Go!**

PC Webopedia responds by displaying a page containing an
explanation of your entered word.

   In Chapter 3 you will learn about search engines that
enable you to search the web and not just an individual
website. You will also learn how to perform searches with
multiple keywords.

Now is a good time to define some of the terms relating to
searching a website, and to searching the web as a whole.

Keyword

> *Text or other keyboard characters entered to a search engine. The engine then displays or 'returns' a list of documents containing the entered text. Typically, the returned list provides links to the indiviual pages, and displays a summary description of each page.*

Website search engine

> *A program that searches a website for keywords entered by the user. It displays or 'returns' a list of web pages on which it found occurrences of the entered word or words.*

Interactive forms

On the web an interactive form is a page containing blank boxes called fields into which you can enter information. Typically, you use forms to specify the particular type of product (for example, a music CD), service (for example, a legal service) or information (for example, train departure times) that you require.

You can also use forms to submit information to a website. When buying a book from an online book shop, for example, you will be presented with a form into which you enter your name and credit card details.

Interactive form

> *A series of fields on a web page that you use to request a specific item of information, or a product or service. You can also use a form to submit information, such as your name and credit card number.*

Exercises 2.8 and 2.9 provide two examples of interactive forms on websites. The first enables you to request a train timetable, the second to specify a PC configuration and view the corresponding price.

Exercise 2.8: Using a form to request a train timetable

1   Visit the Irish Rail website at www.irishrail.ie

2   On the home page, click the link named Timetables.

3   On the Timetables page now displayed, click the **Let's Go** button alongside the line that says Waterford to Dublin.

4   On the next web page displayed, make the selections as shown below and click **Let's Go**.

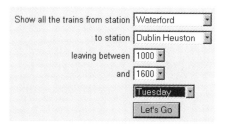

The website responds by listing all train services that match your entered requirements.

Timetable from Waterford to Dublin Heuston
For departure times 1000 - 1600
Tuesdays, Wednesdays and Thursdays

Waterford	1045 1445
Thomastown	1110 1513
Kilkenny(a)	1127 1532
Kilkenny(d)	1131 1541
Munie Bheag	1150 1601
Carlow	1205 1616
Athy	1221 1636
Kildare	1241 1655
Newbridge	1248 -
Dublin Heuston	1330 1737

Cars, sandwiches and personal computers are all examples of highly configurable products whose price varies with the combination of 'ingredients' chosen. In Exercise 2.9 you use a form to specify a PC's configuration and display the resulting price.

Almost all PC manufacturers now sell their products online. Note that the links and link names in the website chosen – Dell UK – may change over time. And relax: this is just an exercise; you are not about to order a new PC!

Exercise 2.9: Using a form to price a customized PC

1   Visit Dell's British website at   ❶ Home & Home Office
    www.dell.co.uk

2   Click the link named Home & Home Office.

3   Click the link for Desktop. You should now see a new page listing a number of PC models. Click any PC model to see a new page that includes a link named Configure & Buy.

4 Click the link named Configure & Buy. 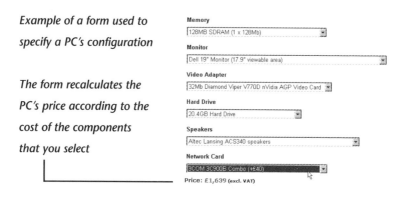 ⊙ Configure & Buy
You should now see a form that lists
several options for such PC components as Memory,
Monitor, Hard Drive and so on.

5 Make and change a number of selections.

Notice that, as you do, the price of the PC, as displayed
at the bottom of the web page, changes accordingly.

Example of a form used to
specify a PC's configuration

The form recalculates the
PC's price according to the
cost of the components
that you select

Memory
128MB SDRAM (1 x 128Mb)

Monitor
Dell 19" Monitor (17.9" viewable area)

Video Adapter
32Mb Diamond Viper V770D nVidia AGP Video Card

Hard Drive
20.4GB Hard Drive

Speakers
Altec Lansing ACS340 speakers

Network Card
3COM 3C900B Combo (+£40)

Price: £1,639 (excl. VAT)

6 When you've finished experimenting with the form, click
the Back button repeatedly to revisit Dell's home page.

About web addresses

In this and the previous chapter you have been entering web
addresses and visiting the associated web pages. A web page is
just another type of computer file. Whereas Word files end in
.doc, for example, and Excel files in .xls, web pages end in
.htm (or, sometimes, .html or .shtml). Let's look at web
addresses in more detail.

To request a web page with Internet Explorer, you need to
know two things:

- The name of the *web server* – the internet-connected computer on which the particular web page is located

- The name of the *web page* (that is, the file) on the web server

Add these two items together and you get what is called a *web address*. Another, more technical, term for a web address is a URL (Uniform Resource Locator).

URL (web address)

The unique address of a web page. It contains the name of the web server and includes (or implies) the name of the particular web page.

Sample URLs

The best way to learn about web addresses is to look at a few examples and discover why they are written the way they are. Here are the URLs of three American websites:

www.latimes.com www.princeton.edu www.cia.gov

In a US web address, the last part of the address – the so-called *suffix* – indicates the type of organization.

For a commercial business (such as the *Los Angeles Times* newspaper), the suffix is .com; for an educational institution (such as Princeton University), it's .edu; and for a government agency (such as the CIA), it's .gov. Not-for-profit organizations use the suffix .org.

Here are some Italian (.it), French (.fr), and German (.de) URLs:

www.yahoo.it www.smartweb.fr www.infoseek.de

www.juventus.it www.renault.fr www.bmw.de

www.ferrari.it www.louvre.fr www.berlinonline.de

In each case, the suffix indicates only the country. Addresses are not categorized by type.

British web addresses end in .uk, but they also include a component to identify the organization type: .co for commercial, .ac for the further and higher education sector, and .gov for government. Here are a few examples:

www.cttraining.co.uk   www.mcc.ac.uk

www.landrover.co.uk   www.cam.ac.uk

www.thisislondon.co.uk   www.ox.ac.uk

www.itn.co.uk   www.bcs.org.uk

www.chelseafc.co.uk   www.amnesty.org.uk

A suffix for primary- and second-level schools, .sch.uk, is becoming increasingly popular.

Other countries that use two suffixes – one for organization type and one for the country itself – are Australia and South Africa. Here are some examples:

www.smh.com.au   www.southafrica.co.za

www.microsoft.com.au   www.icdl.co.za

www.ntu.edu.au   www.unisa.ac.za

www.uwa.edu.au   www.up.ac.za

www.ics.org.au   www.cssa.org.za

www.foe.org.au   www.sarl.org.za

www.deet.gov.au   www.finance.gov.za

www.thesource.gov.au   www.durban.gov.za

Practise your web surfing skills by visiting some of the URLs listed in this topic.

URLs and files

A URL specifies *two* things: the name of the web server and the name of a particular web page on that server. So: where is the web page name in this URL?

www.munnelly.com

Answer: when you enter just the web server name, the server displays the default web page. This is the front or main page of the web site, and is usually called index.htm (or index.html).

The web address of www.munnelly.com, therefore, is really:

www.munnelly.com/index.htm

Here are some other URLs with the name of the default web page included as part of the web address:

www.wit.ie/index.html   www.ucd.ie/index.html
www.ucg.ie/index.html

Notice how a forward slash (/) separates the web page name from the web server name.

When you want to view a web page that is not the front or main page, enter a URL that includes the page name. For example:

www.ucg.ie/departments.html
www.botany.com/narcissi.html
www.refdesk.com/paper.html
www.surfnetkids.com/pocahontas.htm

URLs and folders

On web servers, as on other computers, files are organized into folders. In the four examples above, the web pages are in the main folders of the web servers. But web servers can also store pages in sub-folders or sub-sub-folders. Here are some examples of URLs that include sub-folder names:

www.irlgov.ie/aras/hist.htm

www.lastampa.it/rubriche/ultima/rubriche/lst/cinema/
cinemahome.htm

www.fieldandstream.com/bookstore/fishbooks.htm

www.ozsports.com.au/cricket/commentary.html

A forward slash (/) separates folder names and page names.

Sometimes a URL contains just the web server and folder name – but not the name of the page within the folder. In such cases, your web browser displays the default web page within that folder. Again, this is typically called index.html (or index.htm). For example:

www.tcd.ie/drama/

is really:

www.tcd.ie/drama/index.html

Further practise your web surfing skills by visiting some of the above URLs that contain folder and file names.

When finished, you can close Internet Explorer. You have now completed Chapter 2 of the ECDL *Information and Communication* module.

Chapter summary: so now you know

Websites typically display a navigation bar or *navbar* – a horizontal or vertical list of hyperlinks to the main components of a website – along the top or down the left of each page.

Larger websites help users to navigate by providing one, two or all three of the following features:

- A *site index*, sometimes known as a site map or site guide, is a web page that lists the main contents of a website. It is similar in purpose to the contents page of a printed book.

- A website *search engine* is a program that searches a website for *keywords* entered by the user. It displays or 'returns' a list of web pages on which it found occurrences of the entered word or words.

- An *interactive form* is a series of fields on a web page that you use to request a specific item of information, or a product or service. You can also use a form to submit information, such as your name and credit card number.

A *URL* is the unique web address that contains the name of the web server and includes (or implies) the name of the particular web page. Where no page is specified in a URL, the browser displays the default page, usually *index.htm* or *index.html*.

URLs have at least two parts, separated by a dot (.). In the US, the first part is the organization's name; the second indicates its type. Commercial sites end in *.com*, educational sites in *.edu*, and government sites in *.gov*.

Italian, German and French sites are not categorized by type. Their domain names consist of just the organization name and a suffix indicating their nationality (*.it, .fr,* and *.de*). In the UK, commercial sites end in *.co.uk,* academic sites in *.ac.uk* or *sch.uk,* and government sites in *.gov.uk.* Australia and South Africa also categorize web addresses by organization type.

CHAPTER 3

Finding information on the web

In this chapter

A report published in early 2000 revealed that there were
over one billion pages on the Web, stored on almost five
million websites. Some 85 percent of the pages were in
English, and just over half (55 percent) of web addresses
ended in .com. Faced with such a phenomenal amount of
data, how can web surfers hope to locate individual items
of information of interest to them?

It's not as difficult as it may sound – once you know
how. In this chapter you will discover the techniques for
searching and finding information on the web.

New skills

At the end of this chapter you should be able to:
- Locate information on the web by navigating through
  the categories of a directory site

- Locate information on the web by entering a keyword to search engines and meta search engines
- Perform phrase searches using quotation symbols
- Perform multiple keyword searches using the plus (+) and minus (-) logical operators

New words

At the end of this chapter you should be able to explain the following terms:
- Web directory
- Web search engine
- Web meta search engine
- Logical search

Finding information on the web

I f you are exploring the web for information on a particular topic, four types of websites can help you find what you are looking for:

- **Directory sites**: These are websites that catalogue information on the web according to subject matter.

- **Search engines**: These are websites that search the web for keywords – occurrences of specified words or phrases.

- **Meta search engines**: These are websites that submit keywords to several search engines. In effect, they allow you to use multiple search engines at once.

- **Natural language search engines**: These are websites that accept queries in plain English. For example: 'Who is the Prime Minister of New Zealand?'

In this chapter you will learn about each type of website and discover how you can best use them to find the information you need.

Web directory sites

Directory websites organize information in an easy-to-follow, top-down structure. They tend to be selective, so that only the better sources of information are listed. Unfortunately, the web changes so quickly that directory sites may not always be up to date.

The original and biggest directory site is Yahoo!, where you can browse information by category, sub-category, and, more often than not, sub-sub-category. Exercise 3.1 provides an example.

Exercise 3.1: Finding information on Yahoo!

1 Open Internet Explorer and visit the Yahoo! website at www.yahoo.com

2 Click the link named Astronomy, which is located in the right-hand category column under the Science heading.

Science
Animals, Astronomy, Engineering...

3 You are now shown a new web page. It lists astronomy sub-categories in alphabetic order. Click the link named Planetaria.

- **Pictures** *(86)*
- **Planetaria** *(63)*
- **Radio Astronomy** *(77)*

4 You are shown a third web page. This one lists the websites of some fifty planetaria, including Armagh (at www.armagh-planetarium.co.uk). Click on Armagh Planetarium to visit its web page.

- Allentown School District Planetarium
- Armagh Planetarium (United Kingdom)
- Astronaut Memorial Planetarium and Observatory - Brevard Community College

Exercise 3.1 demonstrates both the range and depth of information available on the web – and the usefulness of directory sites such as Yahoo!

There are country-specific versions of Yahoo! available for a wide range of nations including the UK, Ireland, France, Germany, Italy, Australia and New Zealand. You can link to them from the main site at www.yahoo.com. Other popular web directory sites include About.com and NetGuide.com.

Web directory sites www.yahoo.com, www.about.com and www.netguide.com

Most directory sites also offer a search-engine facility.

Web directory site

A website that lists and categorizes other sites on the web according to their subject matter. Typically, it offers several hierarchical layers, with a listing of website addresses at the lowest level.

Web search engines

A search engine allows you to enter a word or phrase, searches for instances of it, and then displays ('returns') a list of websites that match your entered word or phrase, with a summary of each. You can then click on the one that seems most appropriate to you.

Search engines *do not* search the entire web, but their own smaller, regularly updated list of websites, which typically accounts for about 10 to 15 percent of the total number of sites on the web.

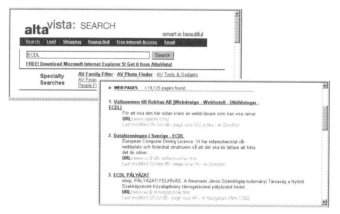

A search for the word 'ECDL' at www.altavista.com returns over 19,000 matching web pages

Web search engines work in a very similar way to the website search engines you met in Chapter 2. The main difference is that they search the web – and not just an individual website.

Search engines frequently find individual pages from websites that have nothing to do with what you are looking for. You can often discover unexpected gems of information this way but be prepared to wade through a lot of irrelevant information too!

Exercises 3.2 and 3.3 provide examples of single keyword searches using search engines. In Exercise 3.2 you use Internet Explorer's default search engine.

Exercise 3.2: Searching with Internet Explorer's default search engine

1 Click the Search button on Internet Explorer's standard toolbar.

> Search   ✕
> ⚡ New   Next ▾ | Cust »
>
> **eXcite**
> Enter the word or words you are searching for:
> `ecdl`
> [Search]
>
> © 1999 Microsoft Corporation.
> All rights reserved.
> Terms of use.
> Privacy statement.

This displays the Search bar to the left of the main window.

(Your Search bar may look slightly different, depending on how Internet Explorer is set up.)

2 In the search box displayed, type the keyword 'ecdl'.

3 Click the **Search** button.

The Search button

You should now see a list of web pages that contain the word 'ecdl'.

You can change Internet Explorer's default search engine by clicking **Customize** at the top-right of the Search bar and selecting a different search engine.

The web offers dozens of search engines. You should explore the various alternatives and choose the one that best suits your needs.

Here are some of the better search engine websites:

www.google.com	www.altavista.com
www.alltheweb.com	www.northernlight.com
www.excite.com	www.hotbot.com

www.webcrawler.com   www.lycos.com

www.go.com   www.snap.com

www.ibound.com   www.mckinley.com

In Exercise 3.3 you visit the Google search engine and use it to find information on ECDL.

Exercise 3.3: Searching the web with Google

1   Visit the Google search
    engine at
    www.google.com

Search the web using Google

ecdl

Google Search   I'm Feeling Lucky

2   Enter the keyword ECDL
    and click the **Google Search** button.

Google responds by displaying a list of web pages that contain your entered keyword.

When your query returns more than a single page of results, search engines provide Next and Previous links at the bottom of each page to allow you to move forwards and backwards through the pages of results.

To print the result of a web search, simply print the results page(s) as you would any other web page.

Web search engine site

A website that enables you to search for material on the web by entering a word or phrase. The search engine returns a list of sites where the specified words were found.

Phrase searches

When searching for a phrase – a sequence of words in a particular order – enclose the phrase within double quotes. Phrase searches are commonly used to find information on people and organizations – even song lyrics. Here are some examples:

"Manchester United"
"Edgar Allan Poe"
"Ministry of Defence"
"Candle in the Wind"

Why do you need to enclose phrases inside quotes? The answer is that if you search (say) for Manchester United rather than "Manchester United", your results may include pages that refer to Manchester Council or United Biscuits.

By placing quotes around a query you ensure that you find only pages that:

- Contain *all* the words of your query

- Contain the words in the *order* in which you type them

Phrase search
A query to a search engine that is placed inside quotes. Only web pages containing all the entered words, in the order entered, are found.

Practise your phrase-searching skills by entering your full name, within quotes, to the Google search engine.

The plus operator

Often you want to search for multiple words that are not necessarily adjacent to one another. In such cases, phrase searches are inappropriate. Instead, use the plus (+) operator.

Suppose, for example, you want to find information about the rules of the card game solitaire. You could enter:

solitaire +rules

Only web pages that contain both words should appear in your results. Note three points about the plus operator:

- You don't need to type the plus operator before the first word that you type in your query.

- Don't leave a blank space between the plus operator and the word following it.

- Leave a blank space after each word.

Here are some other examples:

Word +2000 +templates
Excel +2000 +autosum
ECDL +Cyprus
Recipe +Thai
Shakespeare +Hamlet

You can combine the plus operator with phrases inside double quotes, as the following examples show:

algebra +"square roots"
"Excel 2000" +"keyboard shortcuts"
Volkswagen +Golf +"metallic blue"
"Manchester United" + "David Beckham"
Shakespeare +"Shall I compare thee"
Bogart +Bacall +"The Big Sleep"

Exercises 3.4, 3.5 and 3.6 provide examples of web queries that contain the plus operator.

Exercise 3.4: Using the plus operator on NorthernLight

1   Visit the web search engine
    www.northernlight.com

2   Type the following terms and click **Search**:
    Bizet +Carmen +Domingo

Your results should include web pages that refer to performances of Bizet's opera Carmen that feature singer Placido Domingo.

Exercise 3.5: Using the plus operator on AltaVista

1   Visit the web search engine www.altavista.com

2   Type the following terms and
    click Search:

    "James Bond" +"Sean Connery"

Your results should include web pages about James Bond films that starred actor Sean Connery.

Exercise 3.6: Using the plus operator on Excite

1   Visit the web search engine www.excite.com

2   Type the following terms and
    click Search:

    Barcelona +restaurants +vegetarian

Your results should include web pages listing restaurants in Barcelona that cater for vegetarians.

The plus operator is particularly useful when you find yourself overwhelmed with returns from a web search. By adding one or a few terms, each preceded by the plus operator, you can progressively refine your search so that you receive only the information you need.

The minus operator

Sometimes, you want a search engine to find pages that contain one word – but do *not* contain another word. You can do this using the minus (-) operator.

Suppose, for example, you want information about the solo career of singer Geri Haliwell, but don't want to be overwhelmed by pages relating to her former group, the Spice Girls. You could enter:

"Geri Haliwell" –"Spice Girls"

Similarly, to find information on the post-Beatles career of John Lennon, you could enter:

"John Lennon" –Beatles

If you are a fan of the original Star Trek series, but don't want pages relating to various follow-up series, you could enter:

"Star Trek" –Voyager –"Deep Space Nine" –"Next Generation"

In Exercise 3.7 you search the web for information on Windows 98, and exclude pages that mention the other versions of the Microsoft operating system, Windows 3.1, Windows 95, Windows NT, Windows 2000 or Windows CE.

Exercise 3.7: Using the minus operator on Go

1   Visit the web search engine www.go.com.

2   Type the following and click Go!:
    Windows –95 –3.1 –NT –2000 –CE

Your search results should provide information on Windows 98 only.

In Exercise 3.8 you will search the web for references to Dublin that do not relate to Dublin, Ireland.

Exercise 3.8: Using the minus operator on Looksmart

1   Visit the web search engine
    www.looksmart.com

2   Type the following and click **Search**:
    Dublin -Ireland

    Your search results should list pages that refer to places named Dublin in the USA. Because not every page that refers to the Dublin in Ireland actually contains the word 'Ireland', however, many of your returned pages will relate to Ireland's capital city.

In general, the minus operator helps you to get better results by allowing you to exclude terms that are not of interest. You can combine the plus and minus operators in a single search query.

Logical searches

A search of the web – or of a single website – that contains the plus and/or minus operators is called a logical search.

An alternative way of creating a logical search is to use the so-called Boolean operators instead of the plus and minus symbols. Named after their creator, nineteenth-century mathematician George Boole, these operators include the words AND, OR and NOT, and are typically written in upper-case letters.

The following two logical searches, for example, produce the same results:

"James Bond" AND "Sean Connery"
"James Bond" +"Sean Connery"

Boolean searches have been used traditionally for database searches. On the web, however, the plus and minus operators are supported by more search engines, and are easier to remember and use.

Logical search
> *A web search that uses logical operators, such as the plus and/or minus symbols, to include and/or exclude specified words or phrases from the results.*

Meta search engines

A meta search engine is a search engine that searches search engines. Just enter your word or phrase and the meta search engine submits it to a range of individual search engines, and returns the matching results.

Three popular meta search engines are:

www.dogpile.com
www.mamma.com
www.metacrawler.com

Exercise 3.9: Using the Dogpile meta search engine

1   Visit the meta search engine at www.dogpile.com

2   Enter the following and
    click **Fetch**:
    "access 2000" +sort

Your results will include web pages, found by a range of
individual search engines, that describe sort operations
in the Microsoft Access 2000 database application.

Natural language search engines

The UK and Ireland Ask Jeeves website at www.ask.co.uk is an
example of a search engine that accepts questions in plain
English. Here are some sample queries that you could enter:

Who is the Secretary General of the UN?
Who invented plastic?
Who wrote Catch 22?
What is the currency in Portugal?
What is the temperature in Florence?

A version of the search engine that returns web pages suitable for
younger web surfers, Ask Jeeves for Kids, is at www.ajkids.com.
You can find the US-based site at www.aj.com.

Exercise 3.10: Using the Ask Jeeves natural language search engine

1   Visit the Ask Jeeves website at www.ask.co.uk

2   Type the following question and click **Ask**: How do I find
    an email address?

    Your results screen should look like that shown below.

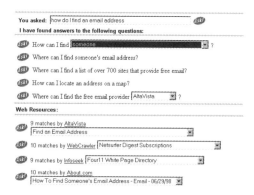

In the top part of the screen Ask Jeeves displays the answers to what it has interpreted as your question. In the lower half it shows the results of entering the words in your question as keywords to various web search engines.

You may now close Internet Explorer. You have completed Chapter 3 of the ECDL *Information and Communication* module.

Chapter summary: so now you know

Directory websites such as Yahoo! catalogue information on the Web according to subject matter. You can locate information on the web by navigating through the various category levels.

Web search engines trawl the web for keywords – occurrences of specified words or phrases – and return a list of websites where the specified words were found.

A *phrase search* is a query to a search engine that is placed inside quotes. Only web pages containing all the entered words, in the order entered, are found. Phrase searches are commonly used to find information on people and organizations.

A *logical search* is a web search that uses logical operators, such as the plus and/or minus symbols, to include and/or exclude specified words or phrases from the results.

If you are overwhelmed with irrelevant returns from a web search, add one or a few terms, preceded by the *plus operator*, to refine your search so that you receive only the information you need.

The *minus operator* helps you get better web search results by allowing you exclude terms that are not of interest. You can combine the plus and minus operators in a single search query.

A meta search engine is one that submits keywords to several other search engines, allowing you use multiple search engines at once.

A *natural language search engine* such as Ask Jeeves accepts queries in plain English.

CHAPTER 4

Taking control of Internet Explorer

In this chapter

In this chapter you will discover how to adjust the appearance and operation of Internet Explorer to suit your working needs and personal taste.

You begin by learning how you can explore the web more quickly by switching off the display of images on web pages. If there is a particular web page that you visit very frequently, you will discover how to make it display automatically each time you start Internet Explorer.

Another convenient feature of Internet Explorer is its ability to save web addresses, and to group saved addresses into folders for easy reference.

Finally, you will learn how to control the display of Internet Explorer's toolbars and various other screen elements, and specify how the application displays web page text.

New skills

At the end of this chapter you should be able to:

- Switch on and off the display of images on web pages
- Save web addresses as favorites
- Organize saved addresses into folders
- Revisit saved web addresses
- Change Internet Explorer's start page
- Display and hide Internet Explorer's standard toolbar and address bar
- Display and hide Internet Explorer's three Explorer bars: Search, Favorites and History
- Adjust the text size of displayed web pages

New words

At the end of this chapter you should be able to explain the following term:

- Favorites

Switching web page images off and on

Web pages with lots of images – or a few large ones – can take an unacceptably long time to display on your computer's screen. Often, these images will be advertisements, company logos and decorative elements that you may regard as inessential – especially if you are the one paying the telephone bill!

Internet Explorer icon indicating a non-displayed image on a web page

Internet Explorer allows you to switch off images, so that you can display web pages more quickly. When you switch off images, Internet Explorer displays only the text of visited web pages, together with a small icon indicating the location of each non-displayed image.

When you arrive at a web page that contains images that you want to display, you can then switch images back on again. Don't be afraid to try this feature – it will save you time and, as Exercise 4.1 shows, it's easy to use.

Exercise 4.1: Switching off images

1   Open Internet Explorer and choose **Tools | Internet Options**.

2   Click the Advanced tab, scroll down the list until you come to the Multimedia category, and then deselect Show pictures.

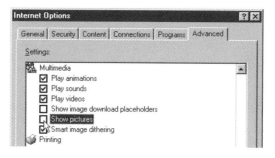

3 Click **OK**.

To display images on all web pages, simply reverse step 2 above.

When images are switched off, you can view an individual image by right-clicking its icon and then choosing **Show Picture**.

Favorites

As you browse the web, you will discover pages that you would like to return to at a later stage. You can tell Internet Explorer to store a web page's address by using the Favorites feature.

Creating a favourite web page saves you needing to remember (or write down) that page's web address. To revisit such a page, you simply click its name from your list of saved favorites – so much easier than retyping its address each time you want to visit it.

Favorites store just web page addresses on your computer, and *not* the actual pages themselves!

Exercises 4.2 to 4.4 take you through the steps of saving web addresses, organizing them into folders, and revisiting them.

Exercise 4.2: Saving a web address

1   Visit the web page whose web address you
    want to save. For example: www.yahoo.com

2   Is the Favorites area displayed to the left   *Displays the*
    of Explorer's main window? If not, click   *Favorites bar*
    the Favorites button on the Standard
    toolbar to display it.

3   At the top of the Favorites area, click the **Add** button.

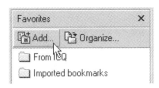

4   You are now shown the Add Favorite dialog box. Accept
    or change the name of the web page whose address
    you are saving. (In this case, Yahoo!).

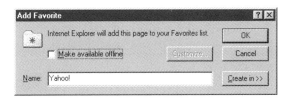

5   Click OK.

Internet Explorer adds the name of the currently displayed
page as the last item in the Favorites list.

Organizing your Favorites

You can group Favorites in folders, so making them easier to find. In Exercise 4.3 you create a folder to store addresses of search engine websites, and then add a number of web addresses to that folder.

Exercise 4.3: Managing favorites in folders

1   Is the Favorites area displayed to the left of Internet Explorer's main window? If not, click the Favorites button on the standard toolbar to display it.

2   At the top of the Favorites area, click the **Organize** button to display the Organize Favorites dialog box.

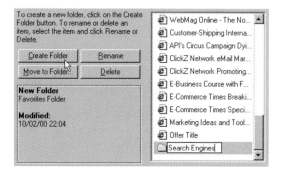

3   Select **Create Folder**, name the new folder Search Engines, and click **Close**.

4   Visit the following website: www.altavista.com

5   At the top of the Favorites area, click the **Add** button.

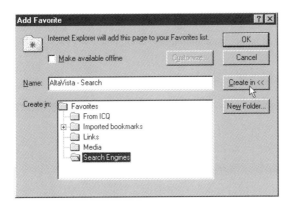

6   In the dialog box displayed, click **Create in** <<, select the Search Engines folder, and click **OK**.

7   Repeat steps 4, 5 and 6 for each of the following other search engine websites:

www.northernlight.com
www.alltheweb.com
www.hotbot.com
www.google.com
www.excite.com

Well done. You now have a folder of saved web addresses.

Revisiting a saved web address

Revisiting a saved web address is easy. In Exercise 4.4 you visit a web address that you added as a Favorite in Exercise 4.3.

Exercise 4.4: Revisiting a saved web address

1   Is the Favorites area displayed to the left of Internet Explorer's main window? If not, click the Favorites button on the Standard toolbar.

2 Scroll down the list of Favorites
until you see the Search Engines
folder that you created in
Exercise 4.3. Click on it.

3 Click a saved web address
from the Search Engines
folder. For example:
www.hotbot.com. Internet
Explorer displays the
associated web page.

Favorites

A list of website addresses stored in Internet Explorer.
Favorites removes the need to remember or retype the
URLs of frequently visited websites.

Changing your start page

Your start page (which Internet Explorer calls the home page)
is the web page that the program visits and displays when
you open Internet Explorer.

Exercise 4.5 shows you how to change your start page.

Exercise 4.5: Changing Your Start Page

1 Go to the page you want to display whenever you start
Internet Explorer. For example: www.munnelly.com

2 Choose **Tools | Internet Options** and select the General
tab. In the Home page area of the dialog box, select **Use
Current** and click **OK**.

To display your preferred start page at any stage, click the Home button on Internet Explorer's Standard toolbar.

Displays your selected start web page

You can restore your original start page – the one set up when Internet Explorer was installed – by selecting the **Use Default** option.

To specify a blank start page – that is, no start page – select the **Use Blank** option.

Screen elements

Internet Explorer's main window is the area in which the application displays the web pages. Surrounding the main window are various screen elements designed to assist you explore and find information on the web:

- Across the top of the main window are the Standard toolbar and the Address bar

- Along the left are the three Explorer bars: Favorites, History and Search

In this topic you will learn more about these screen elements.

Standard toolbar

You have already learnt the purpose of the following buttons on Internet Explorer's Standard toolbar: Back, Forward, Home, Search, Favorites and Print.

Two other important buttons are Stop and Refresh. Click the Stop button if the web page you are trying to view is taking too long to display. The Refresh button re-requests the current web page from the website. Click this button if a web page displays incorrectly or incompletely.

Internet Explorer Standard toolbar

To hide the Standard toolbar, choose **View | Toolbars** and deselect the Standard Buttons option. To redisplay the toolbar, choose **View | Toolbars** again and reselect Standard Buttons.

Address bar

Beneath the Standard toolbar is the Address bar. As you learnt in Chapter 1, this area shows the web address of the currently displayed web page. You can also use it to enter a web address: you type in the required address and then click the Go button or press the Enter key.

To hide the address bar, choose **View | Toolbars** and deselect the Address bar option. To redisplay the Address bar, choose **View | Toolbars** again and reselect the Address bar.

Explorer bars

An 'Explorer bar' is the name that Internet Explorer gives to each of the three screen elements that you can display to the left of the main window. You can display only one at a time:

- To view the Favorites bar, click the
  Favorites button on the Standard
  toolbar, or choose **View | Explorer
  Bar** and select the Favorites option.
  You can then view your list of
  saved web addresses.

- To view the Search bar, click the
  Search button on the Standard
  toolbar, or choose **View |
  Explorer Bar** and select the
  Search option.

- To view the History bar, click the
  History button on the Standard
  toolbar, or choose **View | Explorer
  Bar** and select the History option.

*Internet Explorer
History bar*

The History bar shows the web addresses that you visited in previous days and weeks. To revisit a web page in the History bar, click a week or day, click a website folder to display individual pages, and then click the page icon to display the web page.

You can sort or search the History bar by clicking the relevant arrow next to the View button at the top of the History bar.

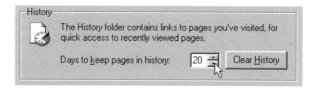

To change the number of days that Internet Explorer keeps track of your visited pages, or to delete the list completely, choose **Tools | Internet Options**, select the General tab, make the required change, and click **OK**.

Text size display

You can change the default size in which Internet Explorer displays text – a very useful feature if you have low or limited vision.

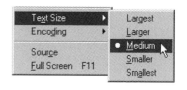

Choose **View | Text Size**, and select the size of text that you want.

You can revert to the default text size of Medium at any stage.

Finally, you can maximize the size of Internet Explorer's main window by choosing **View | Full Screen**.

To revert to normal display, click the Restore button at the top-right of the screen.

Some web pages – such as home pages at www.adobe.com and www.zdnet.com – are designed with fixed-sized fonts, so that using the **View | Text Size** options does not change how they display.

Congratulations. You have now completed the first half of the ECDL *Information and Communication* module.

Chapter summary: so now you know

You can adjust the appearance and operation of Internet
Explorer to suit your working needs and personal taste.

To display web pages more quickly, switch off the
display of images. Internet Explorer displays only the text of
visited web pages, together with a small icon indicating the
location of each non-displayed image.

You can store web addresses, and organize them into
folders for easy reference, using Internet Explorer *Favorites*.
If there is a particular web page you visit very frequently,
you can make it the default *start page*.

Internet Explorer's *Standard toolbar* offers quick access to
commonly used browsing actions. At the left of the main
window you can display any one of the following: the
History bar, *Search bar* or the *Favorites bar*.

Internet Explorer allows you to adjust the size in which
text is displayed on-screen.

CHAPTER 5

e-Mail with Outlook Express

In this chapter

Question: what do most people use the internet for?
Answer: e-mail. It's fast becoming the preferred method of
communication in business, and – because it is so
inexpensive to use – it is also used by friends and family as a
way of staying in touch.

This section introduces you to Outlook Express, the
Microsoft e-mail application. You will explore the
application's main screen elements and discover how to
arrange them to suit your personal taste.

You will also learn how to address, compose and send an
e-mail over the internet, and how to collect and read
incoming e-mails addressed to you.

New skills

At the end of this section you should be able to:
- Start and quit Microsoft Outlook Express
- Display the following four screen elements: Folders list, Message list, Preview pane and toolbar
- Select an e-mail from a message list and display it in the Preview pane
- Select an e-mail from a message list and display it in a separate window
- Compose and send e-mails
- Collect and read incoming e-mails
- Print and delete an e-mail

New words

At the end of this section you should be able to explain the following terms:
- Folders list
- Message list
- Preview pane
- e-Mail collection

Starting Outlook Express

ouble-click on the Outlook Express icon or choose **Start | Programs | Outlook Express**. If your computer has a permanent  internet connection, you are ready to send and receive e-mail messages with Outlook Express.

If you have a dial-up connection, you must dial your internet Service Provider (ISP). Outlook Express may be set up to do this automatically.

If not, you will need to dial your ISP separately.

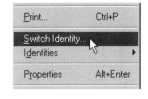

Enter your user name and password (if Outlook Express has not recorded them from the last time that you dialled your ISP), and click **Connect**.

If your computer is used by a number of people, you may have to identify yourself, so that you get your own mail and not someone else's. To do this, choose **File | Switch Identity**, select your name from the list, and click **OK**.

Changing screen Layout

You can change the layout of the Outlook Express screen so that the features you use most often are shown, and those you use very seldom are hidden. This means that two people using Outlook Express might have screens that look very different. For the purpose of the exercises in this module, change the screen layout as directed in Exercise 5.1.

Exercise 5.1: Choosing the display elements

1   Choose **View | Layout** for Outlook Express to present a list of layout options, with a check box beside each one.

2   In the upper area of the dialog box, select the Folder List, Status Bar and toolbar options, and deselect all the others.

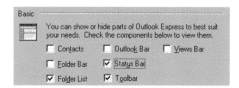

3   In the lower area of the dialog box, select the Show preview pane, Below messages, and Show preview pane header options.

4   Click **OK**.

Your Outlook Express screen should now look like that shown below.

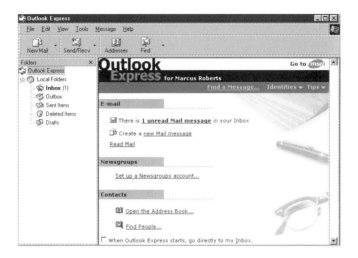

The four layout elements

Let's take a look at the four main screen elements of Outlook Express: folders list, message list, Preview pane and toolbar.

Folders list

The folders list, on the left, shows five folders:

- **Inbox**: This is where all your incoming e-mails – those sent to you by other people – are held.

- **Outbox**: This can hold all your outgoing e-mails – those you have composed yourself – until you send them.

Bold type indicates that a folder contains unread e-mails

- **Sent Items**: This can hold copies of all the e-mails you have sent to other people.

- **Deleted Items**: This is where you put all e-mails – both incoming and outgoing – that you no longer want to keep.

- **Drafts**: This is where you store any e-mails that you have not finished composing.

When a folder contains an unread e-mail, Outlook Express displays the folder name in bold, and shows, in brackets, the number of unread e-mails in that folder.

In addition to the five e-mail folders provided with Outlook Express, you can create folders and sub-folders of your own, and move e-mails in and out of them. You will learn how to do this in Chapter 7.

Folders list

The part of Outlook Express where e-mails are stored and grouped according to type: received (Inbox), waiting to be sent (Outbox), already sent (Sent Items), marked for deletion (Deleted Items), and stored for later editing (Drafts). Users can create additional folders and sub-folders for further organizing their e-mails.

Message list

When you click any folder in the folders list, Outlook Express displays the folder's contents in an area on the right of the screen called the message list. This is called 'opening the folder'.

Click on a

folder to

display its

contents

in the

Message list

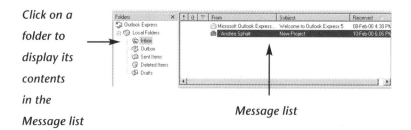

Message list

Outlook Express displays some basic details about each e-mail – the sender or recipient, the subject, and the date and time it was sent or received – and uses the following symbols to provide you with more information:

A *read* e-mail, displayed in light type.

An *unread* e-mail, displayed in bold type.

An e-mail, whether read or unread, with one or more *files attached*. (You will learn about e-mail file attachments in Chapters 6 and 7.)

An e-mail marked as *high-priority*. (You will learn about e-mail priority in Chapter 6.)

Message list

A list of the e-mails contained in the currently selected Outlook Express folder. Outlook Express displays a summary of information about each one.

Preview pane

When you click on an e-mail in your message list, Outlook Express displays the e-mail's contents in an area beneath the message list called the Preview pane.

Click on an e-mail in the Message list to display its contents in the Preview pane

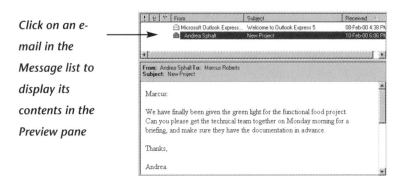

To display a different e-mail in the preview pane, simply click on a different e-mail in the message list.

Resizing the Message list and Preview pane by dragging with the mouse

You can resize the Preview pane and the Message list by clicking on the border between them, holding down the mouse button, and dragging the border up or down.

Preview pane

An area of the Outlook Express screen that shows the contents of the e-mail that is currently selected in the Message list.

If you receive a long e-mail, you may prefer to read it in a separate window. To do this, double-click the e-mail in the Message list.

Reading an e-mail in a separate window

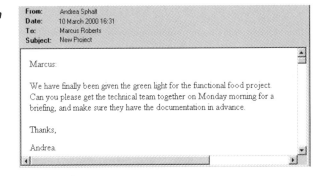

From:	Andrea Sphalt
Date:	10 March 2000 16:31
To:	Marcus Roberts
Subject:	New Project

Marcus:

We have finally been given the green light for the functional food project. Can you please get the technical team together on Monday morning for a briefing, and make sure they have the documentation in advance.

Thanks,

Andrea.

You can then minimize the e-mail's separate window (so that you can come back directly to it at any time), or maximize it (so that it fills the screen). When you are finished with it, close it by clicking the Close button at the top-right of the window. This closes only the e-mail's separate window – and not Outlook Express.

Outlook Express toolbar

The Outlook Express toolbar provides buttons that offer one-click access to the e-mail actions you will want to use most frequently. Different buttons are displayed according to which part of the Outlook Express screen you are working in.

Outlook Express toolbar

Rather than introduce all these buttons at once, we will explain each one as it becomes relevant in this module.

Composing and sending an e-mail

Exercise 5.2 leads you through the steps of composing and
sending an e-mail in Outlook Express.

Exercise 5.2: Composing and sending an e-mail

1　Choose **File | New | Mail Message** or click
the New Mail button on the toolbar.

*The New
Mail button*

Notice how your e-mail address (for
example, marcus@redact.ie) is displayed in
the From: box.

2　Click in the To: box, and type the address of the person
to whom you are sending the e-mail.

3　Click in the Subject: box, and type a brief description of
your e-mail.

4　Click in the main text box, and type the text of your e-mail.

5　When finished typing, choose **File | Send
Message**, or click the Send button on the New
Message toolbar.

The Send button

Congratulations! You have now composed and sent your first e-mail.

What happens to your outgoing e-mail? The answer depends on:

- Your type of internet connection – permanent or dial-up.

- Your selected e-mail sending option – immediate or in a group with other outgoing e-mails.

Outgoing e-mail: permanent internet connection

When you send an e-mail, Outlook Express can transfer it directly to the internet. To set up this option, choose **Tools | Internet Options**, select the Send tab, select the Send messages immediately option, and click **OK**.

If you do not select this option, your e-mail goes only as far as your Outbox folder. It remains there, along with any other outgoing e-mails, until you choose **Tools | Send and Receive | Send All** or click the Send/Recv button on the Outlook Express toolbar.

Don't confuse the Send button on the New Message toolbar with the Send/Recv button on the Outlook Express toolbar.

The Send/Recv button

- **Send button**: This sends the current e-mail to the internet or to your Outbox folder, depending on how Outlook Express is set up.

- **Send/Recv button**: This sends all e-mails in your Outbox folder to the internet.

Outgoing e-mail: dial-up connection

As with a permanent internet connection, you can choose to send each e-mail immediately – or store them in your Outbox for sending later.

You would generally choose to hold all your outgoing messages in your Outbox until you were ready. That way, you can view and type e-mail messages without being connected to the internet. You need only dial up your ISP when you are actually sending or receiving the mail, so that you can exchange all your messages (even hundreds of them, to all over the world) in a single local phone call.

Outgoing e-mail and the Sent Items folder

Outlook Express can place a copy of all outgoing e-mails in your Sent Items folder, so that you have a copy of them for future reference. To set this option, choose **Tools | Options**, select the Send tab, select 'Save copy of sent messages in the Sent Items folder', and click **OK**.

Collecting and reading your e-mail

Just as you can send your outgoing e-mails one at a time or all together, you can collect your incoming e-mail as often as you like, either automatically or manually.

You can collect e-mail from the internet in two ways:

- Automatically at specified time intervals. Choose **Tools | Options**, select the General tab, select 'Check for new messages every 30 minutes', and click **OK**. You can change the timing to suit your needs.

- Manually, by choosing **Tools | Send and Receive | Receive All** or by clicking the Send/Recv button on the Outlook Express toolbar.

  Even if you have set up automatic, timed e-mail collection, you can click Send/Recv at any stage to check if any new e-mails have been sent to you.

e-Mail collection: dial-up connection

If you are using a dial-up connection, you will generally use the same phone call to send your outgoing messages and collect any incoming messages. When you choose **Tools | Send and Receive | Send and Receive All** or click the Send/Recv button, that's what happens.

Don't confuse the action of collecting e-mail with the action of reading it. If you have a dial-up internet connection, you can read your e-mail whether you are online or not. You need only go online to collect your e-mail from the internet.

e-Mail collection

The action of transferring e-mails from the internet to your computer. You must be connected to the internet to collect e-mail, but you can read your collected messages whether you are online or not.

e-Mail collection at startup

You can set up Outlook Express so that it automatically collects your e-mails from the internet when you start the application. To do so, choose **Tools | Options**, select the General tab, select the 'Send and receive messages at startup' option, and click **OK**.

If you have a dial-up connection to the internet, you may prefer not to select this option. Otherwise, Outlook Express will attempt to dial-up your ISP every time that you start the application.

Reading an e-mail

Outlook Express places incoming e-mails in your Inbox folder. When you click on your Inbox folder, your message list shows all your received e-mails, with one e-mail highlighted. The text of that e-mail is shown in the Preview pane.

Click once on any other e-mail in the message list to display its text in the Preview pane. Double-click on any e-mail in the Message list to display its text in a separate window.

The same technique applies irrespective of which folder the message is in: open the folder; select the message; read.

Printing an e-mail

To print the currently open e-mail, choose **File |**
Print or click the Print button on the toolbar.

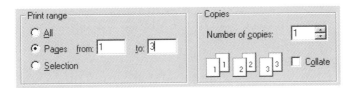

The Print dialog box (which is displayed only if you choose
the **File | Print** command and not when you click the Print
toolbar button) gives you the options:

- **All**: Prints every page of the e-mail.

- **Pages**: To print a group of continuous pages, enter the
  first and last page number of the group.

- **Selection**: Prints only the currently selected text of
  the e-mail.

Other options on the Print dialog box allow you to specify
how many copies you want to print of your selected pages,
and indicate whether you want the multiple copies collated.

Deleting an e-mail

To delete an e-mail, irrespective of whether it is in
your Inbox, Outbox, Sent Items, or Drafts folder, just
click on it in the message list and choose **Edit |**
Delete or click the Delete button on the toolbar.

Deletes current

e-mail

Is the e-mail really deleted? No. Outlook Express places it in the Deleted Items folder. To retrieve the e-mail:

- Click on the Deleted Items folder in the Folders list. Your message list now displays all deleted e-mails.

- Click on the e-mail in the Message list, and hold down the mouse button.

- Drag the e-mail from the Message list to the Inbox or another folder in the Folders list.

Manual e-mail deletion

You can permanently remove all deleted e-mails from Outlook Express by emptying the Deleted Items folder. To do so, select the Deleted Items folder in the folders list, choose **Edit | Empty Deleted Items Folder**, and click **OK**.

Automatic e-mail deletion

If you don't want e-mails to be saved in the Deleted Items folder when you quit Outlook Express, choose **Tools | Options**, select the Maintenance tab, select the 'Empty messages from the Deleted Items folder on exit' option, and click **OK**.

Quitting Outlook Express

To leave Outlook Express:

- Choose **File | Exit**, or click the Close button at the top-right of the Outlook Express window.

Using online help

Like Internet Explorer and other Microsoft applications, Outlook Express offers a searchable online help system. You can search through and read online help in two ways: from dialog boxes, or from the **Help** menu.

Using help from dialog boxes

Exercise 5.3 provides an example of accessing online help from a dialog box.

Exercise 5.3: Accessing online help from a dialog box

1   Choose **Tools | Options,** and click the **General** tab.

2   Click the question-mark symbol near the top-right of the dialog box. Outlook Express displays a question mark to the right of the cursor.

3   Drag the mouse down to the option named 'Play sound when new messages arrive'.

4   Click anywhere on the option check box or name.

> Specifies whether your computer plays a sound when new messages arrive. If you clear this check box, you do not hear any sound, but the Outlook Express status bar and message list will indicate that you have unread messages.

Outlook Express now displays help text telling you about the option. Practise Exercise 5.3 with other dialog boxes in Outlook Express.

Using Help menu options

You can also access online help from the **Help** menu. Choose **Help | Contents and Index** to display the three tabs of the Help Topics dialog box.

Contents tab
This offers short descriptions of Outlook Express's main features.
🕮 *Where you see a heading with a book symbol, double-click to view the related sub-headings.*
❓ *Double-click on a question mark symbol to read the help text.*

Index tab
Reading the material displayed on this tab is like looking through the index of a printed book. Just type the first letters of the word or phrase you are interested in. Outlook Express responds by displaying all matches from the online help in the lower half of the dialog box. When you find the index entry that you are looking for, click the Display button.

Search tab
Can't find what you are looking for in the Contents or Index tabs? Try this tab. When you type a word or phrase and click List Topics, Outlook Express performs a deeper search of the online help. When you find the item you are looking for, double-click on it to display it.

As you search through and read online help topics, you will see the following buttons at the top of the online help window:

- **Hide/Show**: Hides or displays the left-hand pane of the online help dialog box.

- **Back/Forward**: Moves you backwards and forwards through previously visited help topics.

- **Options**: Offers a number of display choices, and enables you to print the currently displayed online help text.

- **Web Help**: Takes you to Microsoft's web-based support site for Outlook Express.

Take a few minutes to look through the Outlook Express online help system. Remember that you will be free to use online help during an ECDL test. When finished, you can close Outlook Express by clicking the Close button or choosing **File | Close**. You have now completed Chapter 5 of the ECDL *Information and Communication* module.

Chapter summary: so now you know

Microsoft Outlook Express is an *e-mail application* that enables you to *compose* (address, write and edit) new e-mails, *send* e-mails (from your computer to the internet), *collect* incoming e-mails (from the internet to your computer), and *read* collected e-mails.

To help you organize your e-mails, Outlook Express contains a built-in *Folders list* in which messages are stored and grouped by type: received (*Inbox*), waiting to be sent (*Outbox*), already sent (*Sent Items*), marked for deletion (*Deleted Items*), and held for later editing (*Drafts*). Users can create additional folders for further organizing their e-mails.

You can collect your incoming e-mails *manually* from the internet, or you can set up Outlook Express to collect them *automatically* each time you start the application and/or at preset time intervals.

You can also tell the application to send each outgoing e-mail as soon as you have finished composing it – or to store outgoing e-mails in your Outbox folder for sending in a group later.

If you have a dial-up internet connection, you can read and compose your e-mail whether you are online or not. You need only go online to send and collect your e-mail. You can keep copies of all outgoing e-mail in your Sent Items folder.

When you open a folder, Outlook Express displays the e-mails that it contains in a *Message list*, together with a summary of information about each one.

Clicking once on an e-mail in a message list displays that e-mail's contents in a *Preview pane* under the message list. Clicking twice displays the e-mail in a separate window.

When you delete an e-mail, Outlook Express places it in the Deleted Items folder. You can empty the Deleted Items folder manually or set up Outlook Express to empty it automatically each time that you close the application.

CHAPTER 6

More about outgoing e-mail

In this chapter

In this chapter you will discover some of the options available for composing and sending e-mails.

You will learn how to copy text into an e-mail from another application, how to check the spelling in your e-mails, how to mark an e-mail as high-priority, and how to send the same e-mail to several people – there are several ways of doing this.

You will also learn how to create a signature and to append it to your outgoing e-mails, and how to attach files to outgoing e-mails – such as word-processed documents, spreadsheets, or photographs of your dog.

New skills

At the end of this chapter you should be able to:

- Copy text into an e-mail
- Check the spelling in an e-mail
- Send the same e-mail to several recipients
- Send a blind copy of an e-mail
- Set the priority of an outgoing e-mail
- Add a signature to outgoing e-mails
- Attach a file to an outgoing e-mail
- Explain why an e-mail may 'bounce', and know what to do about it
- Manage your outgoing e-mail queue

New words

At the end of this chapter you should be able to explain the following terms:

- Cc (Carbon copy)
- E-mail file attachment
- Message priority
- Drafts folder
- Blind copy (Bcc)
- Signature (sig) file
- Bounced e-mail

Copying text into e-mails

Typing text directly into Outlook Express is just one way of composing an e-mail. Another is to reuse previously typed text by copying it from another e-mail (whether received or sent), and then pasting it into the new one.

As Exercise 6.1 shows, you can also copy text into an outgoing e-mail from another application such as a Microsoft Word document. (You should be familiar with Microsoft Word and have a Word document ready to use before attempting Exercise 6.1. Otherwise, you'll just have to take our word for it!)

Exercise 6.1: Copying text from Word to Outlook Express

1 Open Microsoft Word and open the document that contains the text you want to copy into your e-mail.

2 Select the text for copying by clicking at the start and dragging the cursor to the end.

1.0···Overview¶
¶
Many·Internet·service·providers·and·online·services·require·you·to·manually·enter·information,·
such·as·your·user·name·and·password,·to·establish·a·connection.·With·Scripting·support·for·Dial-
Up·Networking,·you·can·write·a·script·to·automate·this·process.¶
¶

Text selected from Microsoft Word

(To select all the text in a Word document, hold down the Ctrl key and click anywhere in the left margin.)

3   Choose **Edit** | **Copy** or press Ctrl+c to copy the selected text to the clipboard.

4   Open Outlook Express and either open the e-mail you want to paste the text into, or compose a new e-mail.

5   Position the cursor where you want the copied text to appear in your e-mail, and choose **Edit** | **Paste** or press Ctrl+v.

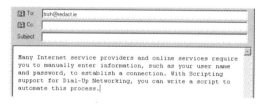

Word text pasted into an outgoing e-mail

Checking your spelling

How's your spelling? Outlook Express can check your spelling and suggest corrections to errors in two ways:

Checks spelling of current e-mail

• When you send the e-mail (the automatic option)

• When you choose the **Tools** | **Spelling** command or click the Spelling button on the New Message toolbar (the on-request option).

If automatic spell-checking is switched on, Outlook Express checks your e-mail after you choose **File | Send Message** or click the Send button on the New Message toolbar.

It uses the same spelling dictionary as Word and other Microsoft Office applications. If you do not have any of these installed on your computer, spell-checking in Outlook Express is not available.

Exercise 6.2: Switching on the spellchecker

1   Choose **Tools | Options** and click the Spelling tab.

2   Select the following two options, and click **OK**: Always check spelling before sending, and Suggest replacements for misspelled words.

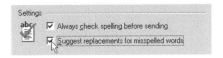

Subsequently, when you send an e-mail, you will be alerted to any word in your e-mail that Outlook Express does not recognize, and offered some alternatives. (Not all unusual spellings are wrong, however, and not all usual spellings are right.)

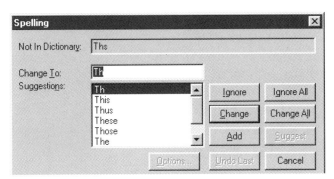

You can **Ignore** the alert, **Change** the problem word to the alternative highlighted, or **Add** the word that caused the problem to the dictionary, so that it does not cause any further alerts.

Finding an e-mail address

You've seen that sending an e-mail is easy, provided you know the e-mail address of the person you are writing to. Where do you find these addresses? There are five main sources: business cards, incoming e-mails, websites, the Find People option, and the Internet Explorer address book:

- **Business cards**: Most people in business today include their e-mail address on their business cards. (Some include *only* their e-mail address – they don't want to be contacted any other way!)

- **Incoming e-mails**: Many of the people you want to send e-mail to have already been in contact with you. Simply go to your Inbox, find an e-mail from the right person, copy their address to the clipboard and paste it into your e-mail.

- **Websites**: If you know the organization to which the person belongs, find its website. Many of them (particularly colleges and government agencies) include e-mail directories.

- **Find People option**: Outlook Express provides an option that lets you quickly locate e-mail addresses from web-based directories.

Choose **Tools | Address Book** and select the **Edit | Find People** button.

From the Look in: drop-down list, select a directory service.

Type the name of the person you are looking for, and click **Find Now**.

This feature works only when you are connected to the internet. (And it's not guaranteed to find the person you want.)

- **Address Book**: An Outlook Express feature that enables you to record e-mail addresses for easy reference. (You will learn about the address book in Chapter 8.)

e-Mailing multiple recipients

You can send an e-mail to more than one person. There are three ways of doing this: several equal recipients, one main recipient with copies to others, and blind carbon copy. You use each for different purposes.

Several equal recipients

If you want to send the e-mail to several people, enter each of their e-mail addresses in the To: box, separated by a comma or semi-colon. To make a string of multiple addresses easier to read, include a space after each comma or semi-colon.

Multiple To: recipients

One main recipient, with copy to another

To send a copy of the e-mail to another person, enter their e-mail address in the Cc: (carbon copy) box. Generally, you use the Cc: box to enter the e-mail address of other recipients you think should see this e-mail as a matter of courtesy or organizational procedure.

Multiple Cc: recipients

Cc is like that: it conveys those kinds of subtle but powerful messages that make office life exciting. You can enter as many e-mail addresses as you want in the To: box and in the Cc: box.

Cc: (e-mail carbon copy)
A field in an e-mail header where you can enter the addresses of people to whom you want to send a copy of the e-mail.

Blind carbon copying

With blind copying, you send a copy of the e-mail to the second person, without the main recipient knowing about it. Before doing this, you need to reveal the Bcc: box by choosing **View | All Headers**. The Bcc: box is shown on all e-mails you subsequently compose, until you turn it off (by choosing **View | All Headers** again).

You simply enter in the Bcc: box the e-mail address of anyone you want to blind-copy the e-mail to. Note that:

- Bcc recipients know the names of the To and Cc recipients.

- The To and Cc recipients do not know the names of the Bcc recipients.

- The Bcc recipients do not know each other's names.

To: and Bcc: recipients

Bcc sends even more subtle messages than Cc. Let's say you send an e-mail to Trish and Bcc Peter. This has the following effects:

- Trish (To recipient) gets the e-mail.

- Peter (Bcc recipient) learns that Trish got the e-mail (and sees what the e-mail was).

- Trish is not aware that Peter knows that she got the e-mail, or what was in it.

- Peter knows that Trish doesn't know that he knows.

- Peter knows that you don't want Trish to know that he knows.

Fun, isn't it? Again, you can enter as many e-mail addresses as you wish in the To: box and in the Bcc: box, and you can include both Cc and Bcc recipients in the same e-mail.

Bcc: (e-mail blind carbon copy)

A field in an e-mail header that enables you to copy an e-mail to other recipients. Bcc: recipients can view addresses in the To: and Cc: fields, but not addresses in the Bcc: field. To: and Cc: recipients cannot view any addresses in the Bcc: field.

Mass e-mail and blind carbon copying

A common use (abuse?) of the Bcc: field is for the sending of mass e-mails that advertise products or services.

The sender places *all* the recipients' addresses in the Bcc: field, so that no one recipient knows who else also received the e-mail. Should the e-mail fall into the hands of a competing company, they are unable to view the sender's list of clients and prospects. In the To: field, the sender types his or her own e-mail address.

Every e-mail you send must have at least one address in the To: box; otherwise, it will 'bounce' back to you. (Bounced e-mails are explained later in this chapter.)

Attaching files to e-mails

e-Mails are generally short text messages. But suppose you want to send a family photograph to your uncle, a spreadsheet to your accountant, a PowerPoint presentation to head office, or a beautifully formatted word-processed document to your tutor? Easy: you send it as an *attachment* to your e-mail message.

To learn how to attach a file to an e-mail, follow the steps in Exercise 6.3.

Exercise 6.3: Sending an attachment

1   Compose your e-mail in the normal way.

2   Choose **Insert | File Attachment** or click the Attach button on the New Message toolbar.

Attaches file to current e-mail

3   In the Insert Attachment dialog box, locate the file you want to attach to your e-mail, and click **Attach**.

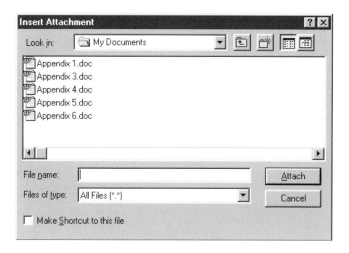

Outlook Express adds a line in the e-mail header to show the attachment file name and file size. To attach multiple files, repeat steps 2 and 3 above.

4 Click **Send** to send the e-mail with its attachment.

Remember that the person who receives your attached file can work with it only if they have the appropriate software application.

e-Mail file attachment

A file, typically a formatted file such as a Word document, that is appended to and sent with an e-mail.

e-Mail priority

All the e-mail you send is important, right? But some of it is more important than others, and you want to make sure that the recipient knows it. Exercise 6.4 shows you how to mark an outgoing e-mail as high-priority.

Exercise 6.4: Sending a high-priority e-mail

1 Compose the e-mail in the usual way.

2 Choose **Message | Set Priority | High**.

3 Choose **File | Send Message** or click the Send button.

High-priority e-mails (incoming or outgoing) are identified by a red exclamation mark. Use the high-priority setting sparingly. If every e-mail you send is high priority, they will all be treated in the same way.

E-mail priority indicators

You can also send e-mails with a low-priority setting in exactly the same way. But who wants to do that? (Low-priority e-mails are identified by a blue down arrow.)

The priority of an e-mail does *not* affect the speed with which it is transmitted over the internet or an internal e-mail network.

You can also change the priority of e-mails you have received. This is a useful way of highlighting e-mails that you want to come back to at a later stage.

e-Mail message priority

An indication to an e-mail recipient of a message's urgency, typically represented by a coloured symbol. The priority of an e-mail has no impact on the speed with which it travels over the internet or private network.

Bounced messages

If you send an e-mail to someone and, for whatever reason, it cannot be delivered, you usually receive a message to that effect. Such e-mails are said to 'bounce' – you send them out; they bounce right back.

The most likely reason for an e-mail bouncing is that you have typed an incorrect address: did you spell it correctly? Did you put in all the right punctuation? Did you put in a hyphen (-) instead of an underscore (_)?

Bounced e-mail

An e-mail that, for whatever reason, fails to reach its recipient, and is returned to its sender with a message to that effect.

Occasionally, your e-mail fails to get through and you don't get any message to that effect. While this is rare, it does happen. Don't assume that because you sent the e-mail, the recipient definitely received it. If it's that important, ask them to acknowledge receipt, either in your e-mail, or automatically. Exercise 6.5 shows you how.

Exercise 6.5: Requesting a receipt

1   Compose a new e-mail in the normal way.

2   Choose **Tools | Request Read Receipt**.

3   Send the e-mail as normal.

When the e-mail is received and opened by its recipients, they are informed that you have requested confirmation. They can choose to send the confirmation or not, but they don't have to do any work – they just click **Yes**.

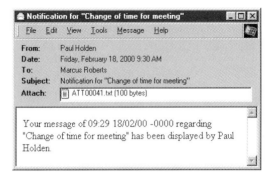

You then get a message like the one above.

Your e-mail signature

When you compose an e-mail, you may want to finish it off with a small block of text as a signature. The easiest and most efficient way to do this is to create a *signature* (sometimes known as a signature file or a sig file). Outlook Express will append this to your outgoing e-mails – either automatically to all e-mails or only to ones that you select.

Most people include their name and contact details. Some add an advertising slogan, a short message, or a link to their website. You can also create different signature files for different purposes.

Creating a signature

Follow Exercise 6.6 to learn how to create an e-mail signature file.

Exercise 6.6: Creating your signature

1   Choose **Tools | Options**, select the Signatures tab and
    click **New**.

2   Click the Text button, and in the text box enter your name,
    address, telephone number and other contact details.

3   Select the 'Add signatures to all outgoing messages'
    checkbox, but do not select the 'Don't add signatures to
    Replies and Forwards' checkbox.

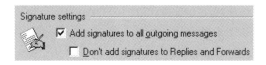

4   Click **OK**.

Outlook Express automatically appends your signature to all
subsequent e-mails you compose and send.

If you want to be more selective, do not select the 'Add
signatures to all outgoing messages' checkbox, as in step 2 of
Exercise 6.6 above. Instead, when you have composed the e-
mail, position the cursor at the point in the e-mail where you
want the signature to appear and choose **Insert | Signature**.

Alternative signature files

To create a second (or a third
...) signature file, choose **Tools
| Options**, and select the
Signatures tab. Then click

New, and proceed exactly as when you created your first
signature file.

   Choose which of your signatures you want to be the
default by clicking it and selecting **Set as Default.** Finally,
click **OK**.
If you have created more than one signature file, and you
subsequently choose **Insert | Signature**, you are offered a
choice from those available.

Renaming your signature file

You can rename your signature files, so that it is easier to
identify the right one for the circumstances. You might have
a signature file called business, one called personal, and one
called family, for example. Or one for your team and another
for head office.

   To do this, choose **Tools | Options**, and select the
Signatures tab. Next, click the signature file you want to
rename, and select **Rename**. Then enter the new name for
the file. Do the same for the other files you want to rename.
When finished, click **OK**.

Editing a signature file

To edit your signature file, choose **Tools | Options**, and select the Signatures tab.

Your signature files are listed. Select the one you want to change by clicking it. Then make whatever changes you want, by adding, deleting, or overwriting the existing information. When finished, click **OK**.

Signature (sig) file

An appendage at the end of e-mails. Typical contents include full name, occupation or position, phone and fax numbers, and e-mail and website addresses. Some people also include a favourite quote, company slogan or short personal statement.

The Drafts folder

If your e-mails are held in your Outbox folder until you click the Send/Recv button, you have the luxury of being able to change your mind.

You can delete an e-mail in the Outbox in the same way as any other e-mail. You select it in the message list, and do any of the following: click the Delete button on the toolbar, choose **Edit | Delete**, or press the Delete key.

Alternatively, you might want to move the e-mail into the Drafts folder while you think about it some more.

Saving e-mail to the Drafts folder

The Drafts folder is where you keep your half-finished thoughts, your letters of resignation and your job applications, until you are sure that they are right and you want to send them.

To put a new e-mail into the Drafts folder, compose the e-mail as normal and choose **File | Save**. To revisit an e-mail in the Drafts folder, open the folder, select the e-mail in the Message list, and double-click it to open it. You can then make any changes or additions, and either save it again to the Drafts folder, or send it.

You can also move an e-mail directly from the Drafts folder to the Outbox by dragging it from the Message list to the Outbox in the Folders list.

Drafts folder

> *An area within Outlook Express where you can store e-mails that you are not yet ready to send. You can open and edit e-mails in the Drafts folder, as required.*

Text size display

You can change the default size in which Outlook Express displays text – a very useful feature if you have low or limited vision.

Choose **View | Text Size**, and select the size of text that you want. You can revert to the default text size of Medium at any stage.

When finished, you can close Outlook Express. You have now completed Chapter 6 of the ECDL *Information and Communication* module.

Chapter summary: so now you know

You can *copy text* from a word processor or other application to an e-mail in Outlook Express, and *spellcheck* your e-mail messages as you would a document in Microsoft Word.

You can address an outgoing e-mail to *multiple recipients* – as equal addressees (To:), as *carbon copied* addressees (Cc:), or as *blind carbon copy* addressees (Bcc:). Bcc: recipients can view addresses in the To: and Cc: fields, but not addresses in the Bcc: field. To: and Cc: recipients cannot view the addresses in the Bcc: field.

When sending an e-mail to several people, separate each e-mail address by a comma or semicolon. You can optionally include a space after each comma or semicolon, to make the addresses easier to read.

You can flag your messages as *high* or *low priority*. This indicates the message's urgency to the recipient, but has no impact on the speed with which it is sent over the internet or private network.

You can append a *signature file* to your outgoing messages, and choose a different signature file for different audiences. Typical signature contents include full name, occupation or position, phone and fax numbers, and e-mail and website addresses. Some people also include a favourite quote, company slogan or short personal statement.

You can *attach* formatted files – such as pictures, spreadsheets and word-processor documents – to your e-mails.

A *bounced e-mail* is an e-mail that, for whatever reason, fails to reach its recipient, and is returned to its sender with a message to that effect.

The *Drafts folder* of Outlook is where you can store messages that you are not yet ready to send.

CHAPTER 7

More about incoming e-mail

In this chapter

In this chapter you will explore some of the options available with incoming mail.

You will learn how to forward received e-mails to other people, how to send replies to the sender or to everyone who received the original e-mail, and how to copy text between e-mails or from an e-mail to a word processor or other application.

You will also discover how to open any file attachments that you receive, and how to save or delete them.

Another topic covered is mail folders – how to create new ones of your own, how to sort the e-mails they contain in different ways, and how to search through your mail folders for specific e-mails.

New skills

At the end of this chapter you should be able to:
- Forward a received e-mail to another person
- Reply only to the sender of an e-mail
- Reply to all the recipients of the original e-mail
- Copy text between e-mails, and from an e-mail to another application
- Open, save, and delete file attachments
- Create and delete mail folders
- Transfer e-mails between mail folders
- Search in your mail folders for a particular e-mail

New words

At the end of this chapter you should be able to explain the following terms:
- e-Mail forwarding
- e-Mail reply to sender only
- e-Mail reply all

Actions with your incoming e-mail

I n Chapter 5 you learnt how to display a received e-mail from your Message list by clicking on it once (to view it in the Preview pane) or twice (to view it in a separate window). In this chapter you will discover the various actions that you can perform on a received e-mail. In summary, these are:

- Forward it to someone else

- Reply only to the person who sent it

- Reply to the sender – and to any other people who also received the message

- Copy text from it to an outgoing e-mail, or to Microsoft Word or to another application

- Open, save or delete any files it may have attached to it.

Forwarding an e-mail

If you receive an e-mail that you want to pass on to someone else, the simplest way is to forward it. Follow Exercise 7.1 to discover how.

Exercise 7.1: Forwarding an e-mail

1 Select the e-mail you want to forward from your
Message list by clicking on it once or twice.

Forward

2 Choose **Message | Forward** or click the
Forward button on the toolbar.

Forwards current e-mail

Outlook Express opens a window that
looks like a window for creating a new e-mail, with two
differences:

• The Subject: box shows the subject of the original e-mail, preceded by the abbreviation Fw:

• The original e-mail is shown and identified.

Area for entering your comments with the forwarded e-mail

Text of received e-mail for forwarding

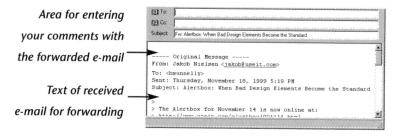

3 In the To: box, type the address of the person to whom
you want to forward the e-mail.

4 In the message area, add text of your own. (It is helpful
to the recipient if you clearly distinguish your own
comments from the original message.)

5 Click **Send**.

e-Mail forwarding

*The act of passing to another person an e-mail that you
have received. You typically include some comments of
your own in the forwarded e-mail.*

Replying to sender only

When you receive an e-mail message, you can send a reply either to the person who sent it to you (only), or to all the people who received the original e-mail.

Most often, you will want to reply only to the person who sent you the e-mail. Exercise 7.2 shows you how.

Exercise 7.2: Replying to the e-mail sender only

1 Select the e-mail you want to reply to from your Message list by clicking on it once or twice.

2 Chose **Message** | **Reply to Sender** or click the Reply button on the toolbar. The window that opens up looks like the window for creating a new e-mail, with two differences:

Replies only to sender of the current e-mail

- The To: box and the Subject: box are already completed.

- The original e-mail message is shown and identified.

Area for entering reply

Text of received mail you are replying to

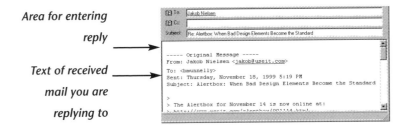

You can edit the Subject: box if you wish. You can also remove all or part of the original e-mail to which you are replying.

3 Enter the text of your reply in the message box, above the words 'Original Message'.

4 Click **Send**.

Remember, it's not very helpful to get a single word reply to an e-mail ('Yes', or '4.30'). The person who reads it could have sent hundreds of e-mails, and could be reading your reply several days later. That's why including the original message with your reply is a good idea.

However, if the original message is very long, and your answer is 'yes', it is helpful to cut out those parts of the original message that do not require a response, so that it becomes very obvious what you are agreeing to.

e-Mail reply to sender only

The act of replying to a recieved e-mail. Only the person who sent you the e-mail gets your reply. The reply typically includes the text of the original e-mail.

Replying to all recipients

The Reply All option enables you to reply to an e-mail, with your reply going to *everyone* who received the original message. You use it in exactly the same way as the Reply (to sender only) function.

Replies to sender and all other recipients of the current e-mail

You will find this feature particularly useful when working with a number of people on a project (drawing up a contract, for example), or discussing something that requires unanimous agreement (to schedule a meeting, for example).

To use this option with a received e-mail, choose **Message |
Reply to All** or click the Reply All button on the toolbar.

e-Mail reply all

*The act of replying to a recieved e-mail. Everyone who
recieved the original e-mail also gets your reply. The reply
typically includes the text of the original e-mail.*

Copying and moving the text of a message

You can reuse the text of one e-mail in another e-mail, or in
another application such as Microsoft Word. And you can
move text around within the same message. Practise your
text-moving skills with Exercises 7.3 and 7.4.

Exercise 7.3: Copying e-mail text within Outlook Express

1   Open an e-mail, or compose a new one.

2   Select the text you want to copy by clicking at the start
    of the text and dragging the cursor to the end.

3   Choose **Edit | Copy** or press Ctrl+c.

4   Go to where you want to insert the copied text, either
    within the same e-mail or in another e-mail.

5   Choose **Edit | Paste**, or press Ctrl+v.

Exercise 7.4: Copying e-mail text into another application

1. As in Exercise 7.44, select the text you want to copy and press Ctrl+c.
2. Open the second application (such as Microsoft Word), position the cursor where you want the copied text to appear, and press Ctrl+v.

In each case, you can move the text in question (that is, delete it from its original location and insert it in its new location), by choosing **Edit | Cut** instead of **Edit | Copy**, or pressing Ctrl+x instead of Ctrl+c.

Deleting text

To delete text, select the text you want to delete, and do any of the following: choose **Edit | Cut**, press Ctrl+x, or press the Delete key.

Receiving file attachments

Most e-mails are simple, self-contained text messages. Some, however, come with files attached – spreadsheets, formatted documents, presentations, graphics, or audio files, for example. You can identify an e-mail with a file attachment as follows:

- In the Message list, it is shown with a paper-clip icon.

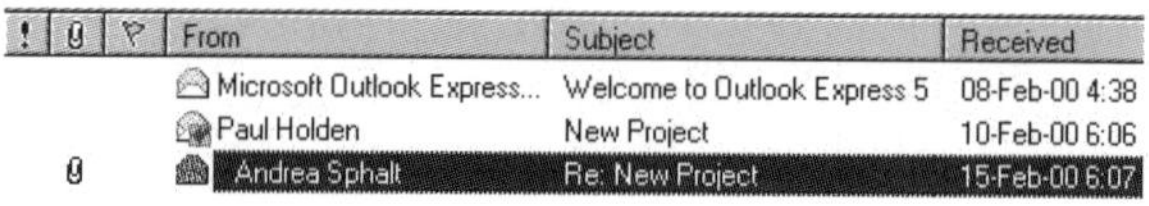
From
Subject
Received
Microsoft Outlook Express...
Welcome to Outlook Express 5
08-Feb-00 4:38
Paul Holden
New Project
10-Feb-00 6:06
Andrea Sphalt
Re: New Project
15-Feb-00 6:07

- In the Preview pane, the e-mail header shows a paper-clip icon.

- If displayed in a separate window, the e-mail header shows an Attach: box, with the name and size of the file.

Opening attachments

You can open a file attachment only if you have an application that is capable of opening it. If someone sends you an attachment that was created in an application that is not installed on your computer (or even a different version of a program that is installed), you may be unable to open it.

You can open an attached file in either of two ways:

- If viewing the e-mail in the Preview pane, click the paper-clip icon in the e-mail header to  display the file name, and then select the file name from the pop-up menu.

- If viewing the e-mail in a separate window, double-click the file name in the Attach: box.

Saving attachments

You can save an attached file in any of the following ways:

- Choose **File | Save Attachments**. (This command is available whether you are viewing the e-mail in the Preview pane or in a separate window.)

- In the Preview pane, click the paper-clip icon in the e-mail header and choose **Save Attachments**.

- In a separate e-mail window, right-click the file name in the Attach: box, and choose **Save As** from the pop-up menu.

In each case, you specify where on your computer you want to save the file, accept or change the file name, and click **Save**.

If you open an attachment and do not save it, you can subsequently open it only from within Outlook Express. If you save it, you can subsequently open it from within Outlook Express and from the relevant application.

If you save an attachment and subsequently delete it, you will not be able to open it *either* from within Outlook Express or from within the application. And if you delete the e-mail without first saving the attachment, the attachment is also deleted.

Careful: attachments can be dangerous

Files attached to e-mail messages are among the most common ways of spreading computer viruses. For this reason, you should install a virus protection application on your computer that scans incoming e-mail attachments.

Using e-mail folders

Once you start using e-mail, you'll probably get a lot of it. Some of it is important at the time, but has a short shelf-life ('Meet you for lunch' 'OK'). Some of it you need to keep for reference (the minutes of the project meetings). Some of it is simply junk mail. How do you keep it organized so that you can find what you want, when you want it? You create *mail folders*, that's how!

Exercise 7.5: Creating a new mail folder

1 Choose **File** | **New** | **Folder**.

2 Type the name you want to give the new folder.

3 Click on the name of the folder in which you want your new folder to be located.

   • If you want it to be at the same level as the Inbox, Outbox and other main folders of Outlook Express, click Local Folders.

   • If you want it to be a sub-folder of an existing folder such as your Inbox, click that folder.

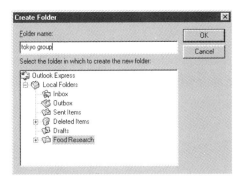

4 Click **OK**.

Transferring e-mails between folders

As Exercise 7.6 demonstrates, you can transfer an e-mail from one folder to another.

Exercise 7.6: Moving an e-mail from your Inbox to another folder

1　Open your Inbox folder and, in the message list, select the e-mail you want to move.

2　Choose **Edit | Move to Folder**.

3　Click the folder into which you want to move the message.

4　Click **OK**.

Alternatively, click the e-mail in the message list, and drag it to the folder in the folder list on the left of the screen. What folder do you use for the junk mail and last week's invitations to lunch? Deleted Items, of course!

If you choose **Edit | Copy to Folder** in Exercise 7.6 above, the e-mail will be copied to the second folder – it will appear in both folders.

Deleting a mail folder

Be careful. It is possible to delete a mail folder, but you can't change your mind. The folder and all its contents will disappear forever. Follow the steps in Exercise 7.7 to discover how.

Exercise 7.7: Deleting a folder

1   In the folders list, click to select the folder you want to delete.

2   Choose **File | Folder | Delete** or click the Delete button on the toolbar.

3   You are asked to confirm that you really do want to delete it.

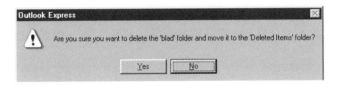

4   Click **Yes**.

Searching for specific e-mails

You know that someone – you can't remember who – sent you details of a new MP3 music player. Your friend in Australia sent you a message sometime around Christmas. You need to see all the replies you received to your mail on the subject of tomorrow's meeting. How do you find what you want?

The quickest way of finding these needles in your e-mail haystack is to use the Find Message function. Exercise 7.8 provides an example.

Exercise 7.8: Finding a particular e-mail

1   Choose **Edit | Find | Message** or click the Find button on the toolbar.

2   If you know which folder the message is in, click **Browse** and select that folder for the Look in: box.

If you're not sure where it is, choose Local Folders and select the Include sub-folders checkbox.

3   Fill in whatever you know about the message – who it was from (or, if you sent it, who it was to), the subject, or some word or phrase in the text of the message. You don't have to use full words: even a single letter is enough. You can also specify a range of dates.

4   Click **Find Now**. Outlook Express displays a list of messages that satisfy your criteria.

When you see the one you want, double-click it to open it.

Sorting messages in a folder

An alternative way of finding a particular message is to sort the items in the folder. If you sort your Inbox alphabetically by the name of the sender (the From field), you can find all the messages from a particular person, for example. Or you can find your most recently received messages by sorting it on the Received field.

Exercise 7.9: Sorting the contents of a mail folder

1 Click your Inbox in the folders list.

2 In the message list, click the word From in the header. Outlook Express sorts your messages alphabetically by the name of the sender.

3 Click on the word From again. Outlook Express re-sorts the messages into reverse alphabetic order.

4 Click the Received field in the header. Outlook Express sorts your messages into the order in which they were received. As before, you can reverse the order by clicking Received again.

When finished, you can close Outlook Express. You have now completed Chapter 7 of ECDL module 7, *Information and Communication.*

Chapter summary: so now you know

Outlook Express allows you to perform various actions on e-mails that you receive from others.

You can *forward* an e-mail to someone else, typically accompanied by some comments of your own which you enter in the text area above the original e-mail.

You can *reply to the sender only*, so that just the originator of the e-mail sees your reply. Or you can *reply to all recipients* of the original e-mail.

You can use *copy and paste* to insert the text of a received e-mail in an outgoing e-mail or in another application such as Microsoft Word.

Outlook Express indicates whether an incoming e-mail has a *file attachment*. You can open, save and delete attachments. File attachments may contain viruses, and you should use a reliable virus protection application to scan them.

You can create *mail folders* to keep your e-mails organized, you can sort the e-mails in any folder, and you can use the *Find* function to search for a particular e-mail by sender, receiver, subject, or date.

CHAPTER 8

Address book and contact groups

In this chapter

By now, you have probably noticed that e-mail addresses can be difficult to remember. Some are cryptic (bill@xyz.com); others are complex (bs_p.sales@xy.pqrcorp.co.uk). Even within the one organization, different people use different conventions (billsmith, bsmith, bill.smith, bill_smith, bsmth ...). How do you remember all these addresses?

You don't – you keep them in your *address book*.

In this chapter you will learn how to organize your contacts in your address book, so that you don't have to remember their e-mail addresses and enter them each time you want to send them a message.

You will also discover how to set up contact groups (also called mailing lists), so that you can send the same message to large groups of people in a single operation.

New skills

At the end of this chapter you should be able to:
- Add, change, and delete contacts in your address book
- Create contact groups that can be e-mailed all at once

New words

At the end of this chapter you should be able to explain the following terms:
- e-Mail contact
- Address book
- Nickname (alias)
- Mailing list (contact group)

Your address book

Outlook Express contains an area called an *address book* where you can keep information about the people you communicate with.

You can record all sorts of details about your contacts – obvious things, like their names, addresses, and phone numbers (and e-mail addresses!), and less obvious things, like their birthdays, and the names of their children.

e-Mail contact

A person or organization whose details (such as name and e-mail address) you have recorded in the address book of your e-mail application.

To explore the variety of information that you can record about your contacts, open Outlook Express, choose **Tools | Address Book** or click the Addresses button on the Outlook Express toolbar. Next, click the New button on the address book toolbar, and then choose **New Contact**.

Addresses

Displays address book

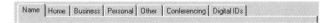

Click successively on the seven tabs of the dialog box, view the various fields available, and, when finished, click **Cancel**.

Address book

> *A feature of an e-mail application that enables you to record details about your e-mail contacts for easy reference.*

Entering contacts

In Exercise 8.1 you will practise entering a new contact to your Outlook Express address book.

Exercise 8.1: Adding a contact to your address book

1   Open your Outlook Express address book by choosing **Tools | Address Book**.

2   Click the New button on the Address Book toolbar, and then select New Contact.

3   In the Name tab, type the first name, last name and e-mail address of one of your contacts.

4   In the Nickname field, type a short, easy-to-remember version of their name (even a single letter). Do not enter any spaces within the nickname.

You can subsequently enter the nickname in the To: field of an e-mail. (It is often called an alias.)

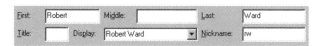

5   Click **OK**.

To create several new contacts in one operation, click **Add** after you type the details of each one. The **Add** button adds new contacts without closing the dialog box. The **OK** button adds the most recently entered contact – and closes the dialog box.

E-mail nickname (alias)

A shortened form of an e-mail address that you can enter in the To: field of a message as an alternative to typing the contact's e-mail address in full.

Contacts: the minimum details

As a minimum, each contact in your address book must contain a first name, a last name, and a display name. All other contact details are optional. The first two you enter; the third is supplied, by default, by Outlook Express.

The display name is the name that appears in the To: field of e-mails that you send to that contact, and in the From: field of e-mails you receive from that contact.

You can change the default display name by typing in a different name or by selecting an alternative from the drop-down list. The drop-down list contains variations of the First/Middle/Last name, as well as anything you typed in the Nickname box or the Company box of the Business tab.

Editing contacts

At any time, you can change the details of a contact or add further details, simply by:

- Choosing **Tools | Address Book** to open your address book

- Double-clicking to select the relevant contact

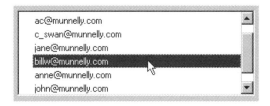

- Overtyping, deleting, or adding the new information

Deleting contacts

To delete a contact, open your address book, select the relevant contact, and do any of the following: click the Delete button, press the Delete key, or choose **File | Delete**.

Adding contact details from e-mail messages

In Exercise 8.1 you learnt how to add a new contact by opening your address book, and entering and saving the relevant details. You can add a new contact in two other ways:

- Display the Inbox or Outbox Message list, right-click on an e-mail, and choose **Add Sender to Address Book** from the pop-up menu.

- When replying to an e-mail, right-click on the name in the To: field, and choose **Add to Address Book** from the pop-up menu.

You can also get Outlook Express to add all reply recipients to your address book automatically as follows:

- Choose **Tools | Options**.

- On the Send tab, select the Automatically put people I reply to in my Address Book option, and click **OK**.

Sorting your contacts

You remember her first name but not her last name? You know the telephone number but not the name of the company? With a normal telephone directory, you'd have a problem. With Outlook Express – no problem. Exercise 8.2 and 8.3 take you through the steps.

Exercise 8.2: Sorting by first name (method 1)

1 Choose **Tools | Address Book** to open your address book.

2 Choose **View | Sort By**.

3 Select the Name, First Name, and Ascending options.

You may have to repeat step 2 to achieve this.

You can then easily find a person by their first name by scrolling through the list.

Exercise 8.3: Sorting by telephone number (method 2)

1   If your address book is not open, choose **Tools | Address Book** to open it.

2   Click the words Business Phone in the header row. Click on the same words a second time.

Note that the order changes with each click, from ascending to descending to ascending again. You can now find the name you want by scrolling to the telephone number you recognize.

Mailing lists (contact groups)

If you regularly use e-mail to stay in touch with your football team, your research group, or your extended family, then you already know that you can send the same message to them by including all their names in the To: or Cc: box. (Remember to separate them with semi-colons, and to have at least one name in the To: box!)

However, after a while, all that typing can get a bit tedious. What do you do? You set up what is generally known as a mailing list but which Outlook Express calls a *contact group*. Exercise 8.4 shows you how to create a contact group and add members to it.

Exercise 8.4: Setting up a contact group

1 If your address book is not open, choose **Tools |
   Address Book** to open it.

2 Click the **New** button and select New Group.

3 Give the new group a name – preferably a short, easy-
   to-remember name.

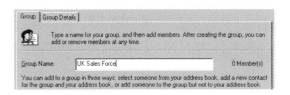

4 Two situations are now possible:

   • The people you want to include in your new contact
     group are in your address book.

   • The people you want to include in your new contact
     group are not in your address book.

   If a person is already in your address book, click **Select
   Members** to view a new dialog box that lists your e-mail
   contacts. For each contact you want to include, click
   their name and then click **Select ->**.

   When finished, click **OK** to return to the main contact
   group dialog box. Now, go to step 5.

   If the people you want to include are not in your
   address book, and you don't want them to be (because
   you never want to address them as individuals), type
   their name and e-mail address and click **Add**.

Continue typing names, e-mail addresses and clicking the **Add** button until you have entered the persons who are not in your address book.

5   When you have finished, click **OK**.

Once you have set up the group, you simply insert its name in the To: field of the message. Outlook Express sends the message to everyone in the group.

Mailing list/contact group

A list of e-mail addresses to which you can send a message in a single operation by entering the list's name in the To: field of the message.

Groups within groups

A contact group may contain the names of other contact groups. For example, your Global Sales group might consist of three groups – the Europe sales group, the US sales group, and the ROW sales group.

An individual may be a member of more than one group. At any time you can change the composition of your group by adding new members (exactly as in Exercise 8.4 above) or removing members (as in Exercise 8.5 on the next page).

Exercise 8.5: Removing members from a group

1 If your address book is not open, choose **Tools |
Address Book** to open it.

2 Double-click on the name of the contact group.

3 Click the name of the person you want to remove, and
click **Remove**.

4 Click **OK**.

If you remove a name from a group, they still remain in your
address book, and in any other group of which they are a
member. However, if you delete (or change) a name in your
address book, it is deleted (or changed) in every group of
which it is a member.

Congratulations! You have now completed ECDL module 7,
Information and Communication.

Chapter summary: so now you know

An *e-mail contact* is a person or organization whose details
(such as name and e-mail address) you have recorded on
e-mail application software. Outlook Express allows you to
record a wide variety of information about your contacts,
spread over seven tabs of a dialog box.

At a minimum, each contact must contain a first name, a
last name and a display name. The first two you enter; the
third is supplied, by default, by Outlook Express. An e-mail
nickname or *alias* is a shortened form of an e-mail address
that you can enter in the To: field of a message as an
alternative to typing the contact's e-mail address in full.

An *address book* is that part of your e-mail application where your contacts are stored for easy reference. You can type contact information into your address book directly, or you can add contact details to the address book from outgoing or incoming messages.

Outlook Express allows you to edit contact details, and to sort contacts according to such headings as last name and phone number.

A *mailing list* or a *contact group* is a list of e-mail addresses to which you can send a message in a single operation by entering the list's name in the To: field of the message. A contact group may contain the names of other contact groups. You can change the composition of a contact group by adding or removing members. An individual may be a member of more than one group.